SERVICE
REBOOT

SERVICE REBOOT

The New Science
of Selling, Marketing,
and Managing Services

By David Selch

Service Reboot

For information about this title or to order other books and/or electronic media, contact the publisher:
Cambrian Publishing
44074 Redwood Centre
Winnipeg, Manitoba, Canada R2W5M3

Cambrian Publishing

www.cambrianpublishing.com
Editors@CambrianPublishing.com

ISBN: 978-1-7751694-1-3 (print)
       978-1-7751694-2-0 (eBook)

Printed in the United States of America

www.ServiceReboot.com

Cover and Interior design: 1106 Design

Publisher's Cataloging-In-Publication Data
(Prepared by The Donohue Group, Inc.)

Names: Selch, David, author.
Title: Service reboot : the new science of selling, marketing, and managing services / by David Selch.
Description: Winnipeg, Manitoba : Cambrian Publishing Canada, [2018] | Includes bibliographical references.
Identifiers: ISBN 9781775169413 | ISBN 9781775169420 (ebook)
Subjects: LCSH: Service industries--Marketing. | Service industries--Management. | Selling.
Classification: LCC HD9980.5 .S45 2018 (print) | LCC HD9980.5 (ebook) | DDC 658.8--dc23

Acknowledgments:

Writing may seem like a solitary effort, but this book would never have been completed without the endless patience and encouragement from my friends and family. There can be no greater praise than, "This is a great book, Daddy."

I have a whole team of publishing and media professionals to make me look smarter and more organized than I really am. My thanks to:

Amy Collins at New Shelves
Michele DeFilippo and Ronda Rawlins at 1106 Design
Kevin Uddenberg at Not Doing Anything
All the folks at Cambrian Publishing Canada

For Debbie

Thank you for marrying me 30 years ago

Contents

Chapter One

That can't possibly be right, can it?

Services.

You know. That little niche that makes up 70% of our economy.

This book is about selling, marketing, advertising, and managing Services.

Services drive the local economy…

68% U.S. Gross Domestic Product contributed by Services

$1.1 Trillion Value of Services supplied by U.S. companies abroad
(That's Trillion, with a "T")

… but we're not preparing our future leaders to think about Service businesses.

3,315 Number of courses offered, collectively, at the top 20 business schools

19 Number of those courses that focus on Service businesses

3 Number of those courses that focus on Services marketing

1 Number that focus on the development of new Services

The vast majority of us are employed in Service businesses...

Percentage of U.S. Jobs in Service industries:

80%

Number of people employed in Service industries:

112 Million

Number of NEW JOBS expected to be created in Service industries over the next decade:

19 Million

…but most researchers pay no attention to the Service economy.

Number of scholarly journal articles discussing Services marketing **as part of a larger Product/Service discussion:**

86,259

Number of journal papers **solely focused** on Services marketing:

76

Number of those that provide tactical direction to managers on **Services advertising:**

19

Number that contain content on selling Services:

1

We know that Services are important to global trade...

· ·

Value of Service-based exports to U.S. economy:
$606 Billion

Trade deficit (in favor of the U.S.) resulting from Services exports:
$179 Billion

…and yet it seems nobody really understands much about them.

Number of pages, collectively, in the top 20 best-selling college-level "Introduction to Marketing" textbooks

6,415

Percentage of pages dedicated to Services:

3%

Most common theme: "Services are different than Products, and so the lessons in this book **don't apply to Service businesses**"

And while we may think we understand Services, we don't even know what we don't even know.

Percentage of corporate sales training manuals, sales methodologies, textbooks, and journal articles still using the **discredited** IHIP model that wrongly suggests Services are

Intangible,

Heterogeneous,

Inseparable, and

Perishable:

99.99%

WAIT! What do you mean by "discredited"?

I'm studying the IHIP model right now in my MBA program, and I go to a VERY good school.

WHAT?

Well, don't take **my** word for it. Take the word of four of the top minds in the marketing field:

Christopher Lovelock
Everett Gummesson
Stephen Vargo
Robert Lusch

If you don't recognize their names from your business textbooks, here's some background on them:

Taken as a group, the four are authors of more than 100 business books published in 10 languages in 30 countries.

Not just **academics** at top business schools, they have won industry recognition as **marketing practitioners** in the fields of Banking, Hospitality, IT Services, Publishing, Telecommunications, Business Services, and Retailing.

Collectively, their industry
awards include:

American Marketing Association
Lifetime Achievement (two of these)

Thompson Reuters' World's Most
Influential Minds

Academy of Marketing Sciences
Distinguished Educator

Chartered Institute of Marketing Top 50
Most Influential People

Here's what they had to say
about IHIP in 2004...

The claim that Services are uniquely different from Goods on the four specific IHIP characteristics is not supported by the evidence

INTANGIBILITY: At worst, it does not hold up; at best, it has little or no relevance

INSEPARABILITY: A delineation delusion

INTANGIBILITY: Intangibility emerges as an ambiguous and surprisingly limited concept

INTANGIBILITY: Not a universally applicable characteristic of all Services

PERISHABILITY: Some Services output is durable, and may even be irreversible

INSEPARABILITY: There are far too many separable Services to justify the generalization that inseparability is a distinctive characteristic of all Services

IHIP is not generalizable to all Services

I: myth.
H: myth.
I: myth.
P: myth.

HETEROGENEITY: It is inappropriate to continue to generalize about heterogeneity as being a distinctive characteristic that sets all Services apart from all Goods

PERISHABILITY: Clearly, tangible Goods are perishable, some of them highly so… Bananas rot, bread gets stale and moldy, and cars rust.

We advocate that the strategy of differentiating Goods from Services be abandoned

Numerous exceptions exist to the received wisdom that all Services possess IHIP characteristics

There is still no generally accepted,
positive definition of Services.

The IHIP model is inaccurate,
misleading, and contradictory.

We are explicitly calling
for a new direction.

All quotes excerpted from:

"Whither Services Marketing? In Search of a New Paradigm and Fresh
Perspectives," by Christopher Lovelock and Evert Gummesson,
in the *Journal of Service Research*, August 2004

"The Four Service Marketing Myths, Remnants of a Goods-Based
Manufacturing Model," by Stephen Vargo and Robert Lusch
in *The Journal of Service Research*, May 2004

Well, then.

What these leaders in the field were saying is that the largest economic contributor of jobs, revenues, and profits is something we don't understand and can't even manage to define.

Their edict, "We are explicitly calling for a new direction" ignited an explosion of new research.

This book collects the new approaches since 2004—theories and practices too new to be in current textbooks. It shares a fresh, powerful definition of Services that explains *why* and *how* selling Services is different from selling manufactured Products.

Those differences affect everybody who has a hand in generating revenue: salespeople, their managers, executives with budgets to meet, and the HR professionals who hire and train them. This book has chapters for each of you.

Intrigued? Let's begin.

Chapter Two

YIKES!

The developed world's economy is founded on Service businesses. Not only do Services account for the vast majority of current jobs, but it's expected that 30% of growth will come from increases in the Service industries, and especially new Services—Services that we can't even imagine today.

Yet only 4 of the top 20 business schools teach courses dedicated to Services Management; only one of these is focused on innovating *new* Services.

Even if instructors wanted to focus on Services in their curriculum, less than 3% of the pages in introductory marketing texts with copyright dates after 2012 are dedicated to Services.

And 100% of that 3% is delivering outdated and incorrect material that has been wrong since the 1960s.

I researched and wrote this book in self-defense over a 25-year career selling and marketing Services. As my average sale size increased from $16 a month for health-club memberships to

$1.6 million for project management, I've never sold anything that you could take a picture of or drop on the floor.

Like any ambitious salesperson, I took my craft seriously, and was always on the lookout for that needle in the haystack: *sales training that applied to Service offerings.*

As a young salesman, trying to support my family by representing a consumer service, every day began with me asking myself the same question: How can I sell more? *This is the book I needed to read.*

After they promoted me to sales manager, I didn't get to ask that question anymore; I was expected to have answers. Each member of my staff asked me what they could do to sell more. Worse, my regional manager asked me what I was doing to help. *This is the book I wanted to show them.*

The old question morphed into new forms as my career path bounced me into the marketing department of an international B2B services company. What is our marketing department doing to help us sell more? What should our advertising look like? How can we differentiate ourselves from the 100 other talented firms offering a similar suite of services? *This is the book that answers our questions.*

I thought it would get easier as I moved up the company ladder. But as a Vice President of Sales, my CEO asked me *harder* questions. "Our Marketing budget just became seven figures. How do we measure ROI on that?" and "How does 'thought leadership' translate to 'net revenue'?" In other words, "Are we doing the right things to sell more?" *This is the book to guide C-Suite decisions.*

I was smart enough to know I didn't know the answers, and so I read voraciously, from Brian Tracy's *24 Techniques for Closing the Sale* to Michael Porter's *Five Forces*. Along the way I got an MBA focusing on Marketing.

And what I learned was… nothing.

It seemed that everything covered in my business classes applied to Products, Goods, and Manufacturing: how to reduce the amount of raw stock; how to strategically discount prices to empty warehouses; how to efficiently transport merchandise to a suitable place of sale; and so on. The advertising course taught me the importance of visual hierarchy, stressing that the images in my ad should reinforce my Product's benefits, so that the ad would resonate in the subconscious mind of my buyers.

All good lessons, but none of them applied to *my* world. I sold Services, specifically: Access; Research; Design; Security; Education; Healthcare. I had no raw stock, no warehouses, and could not transport my offerings. My offerings had no form! (Try using Google Image Search to find an appropriate graphic illustrating *research design*.)

At first I thought *I* was the problem… that I hadn't looked hard enough. So I kept reading.

Zig Ziglar and Brian Tracy and Og Mandino and… Well, you get the picture. And since the practitioners didn't have answers for me, I turned to the theoreticians.

What I found wasn't promising. I found peer-reviewed journal papers that sagely told me:

"A Service is what you have when you don't have a Product."

and

"A Service business can be defined as a business that delivers Services as its primary offering, and a Product business can be defined as a business that delivers Goods as its primary offering."

There were even articles, published in respected journals, insisting there was no difference between Goods and Services... That it was just an ontological trick that made it *seem* like there was a difference. For example, you could portray automobile manufacturing as being a service that filled a need for personal transportation, and dry cleaning as being a manufacturing process that took dirty shirts as its raw materials, produced clean shirts as its finished product, with sweat and grime being waste materials discarded during the manufacture.

I couldn't accept that. It seemed to me that there was, fundamentally, something very different between the two charcoal-gray suits hanging in my closet. Virtually identical, one had been purchased at a men's clothing store downtown, and one had been made for me by a tailor on the same block.

To confirm my intuition, I noted that although they were both of equally fine cloth and both tailored to fit me well, *different terms were used to describe them*. One was "off the rack," the other "bespoke," and if nothing else pointed to them being different in character, their respective price tags insisted there was a difference. One business provided me with a Product, the other with a Service.

As a career salesperson, I knew instinctively that there was a difference between selling Products and selling Services. And even if that difference couldn't be quantified, or even defined, others agreed with me, from Lynn Shostack's 1977 paper "Breaking Free from Product Marketing" (the first paper I was able to find that said that marketing Services was different from marketing Products) to Kathleen Mortimer's 2008 paper "Identifying the Components of Effective Service Advertisements."

So I continued doing my research. I became an expert in the (now discredited) IHIP model that suggested Services were Intangible, Heterogeneous, Inseparable, and Perishable, and in the various approaches to "productize" a Service to make it more buyable. Very little of what I read were *answers*. Rather, most authors were still framing the questions and yearning for solutions.

But among the hundreds of papers I read in publications with titles like *The Journal of Service Marketing,* I found these papers:

Whither Services Marketing?
In Search of a New Paradigm and Fresh Perspective
by Christopher Lovelock and Evert Gummesson

and

The Four Services Marketing Myths,
Remnants of a Goods-Based Marketing Model
by Stephen Vargo and Robert Lusch

Do you recognize the authors? If you've ever taken a university-level course on Marketing, then these are the people who either wrote your textbooks or were quoted within them.

In other words, *the world's foremost marketing theoreticians were essentially throwing up their hands and admitting that so little was known about Services marketing, they couldn't even agree on a basic definition of "Services."*

I have to admit I felt better. It seemed that it wasn't just *me* that knew nothing about Services—it was *everybody* that knew nothing about Services.

The light at the end of the tunnel appeared in a tentatively titled paper published in 2006, *Foundations and Implications of a Proposed Unified Services Theory*. In it, the authors, Scott Sampson and Craig Froehle, gave a simple and complete definition of Services and a rule to definitively differentiate between a Product and a Service.

More than just a giving a cogent definition of what a "Service" is, Unified Services Theory provided the basis for intelligent discussion of management's challenges. To quote from Sampson's excellent workbook, *Understanding Services Businesses:*

"Unified Services Theory occurs as a defining principle. It serves to unify, or reveal commonality, among all service businesses. In addition, it forms the basis for a myriad of Service Business Principles—principles which define good business practice in service industries. By understanding what makes a service business a service business, we gain insights into the critical success factors of such a business."

As a theory, The UST was "unified" in that it applied equally to every Service, from locomotive repair to bicycle-courier delivery to museum design to criminal defense. Therefore, lessons learned in one Service vertical could be applied to other Service verticals.

The UST informs business decisions on the four "Ps" of big-M marketing: Product, Place, Promotion, and Price. That is, the decisions made in the C-suite about what business the company is in, how it will bring its offering to market, and how it will succeed against competitors.

The principles of Sampson and Froehle's Unified Services Theory are revealed in the next chapter. If you take away nothing else from this book, reading their clear differentiation between Products and Services will change the way you look at your business.

This book takes the principles of UST and applies them to the little-M marketing department; that is, to the areas of promotion (advertising) and sales, in order to raise and answer crucial business-development questions such as:

- Can a Service really be "productized"? If so, what changes must be made to the Service, and what does the final Product look like?
- Are there differences in "closing techniques" for Products and Services? What about for cold calling? And the steps in between?
- Is it true that a good salesperson can sell anything? Or are different personality traits needed to sell Products than those that are needed to sell Services?

- Why do *all* successful Service sales presentations *always* require an extra step that is *never* required for *any* Product sales presentation?
- How does one advertise something that has no fixed parameters?
- In what ways must the *call to action* in a Service advertisement differ from a Product advertisement to be effective?

This last question is answered by my own research that formed the basis for my Master's thesis, in which I analyzed the calls to action in 734 business-to-business ads in 83 trade journals for 15 quantifiable characteristics.

This research had two goals: Firstly, to see if the principles of UST were reflected in real-world business activities (they are), and secondly, to assemble a set of best practices for Services advertising (the results will surprise you.)

As with Unified Services Theory, the lessons presented in this book are applicable to all Services and useful to all sales/marketing decision-makers, whether the business repairs heart valves, dry cleans clothing, designs airports, transports hikers to the top of a mountain, drills wells, or audits financial records.

This book is for you if you regularly make decisions for a Service business or a business that offers a mix of Products and Services:

- If you are a salesperson or sales manager, this book details the fundamental differences between selling Services and selling Products. It offers new guiding principles—based on UST—for every point in the sales cycle (from prospecting to closing) and explains how your approach must change depending on whether you are selling Products, Services, or a mix of both.

- If you are in the marketing and promotions department, this will provide direction to advertising content, whether that content is displayed on a banner over a trade-show booth or in your Twitter feed.
- If you are in the C-suite, the principles in this book can be applied to create relevant metrics for evaluating the performance of your marketing department and to operate a more effective sales team.
- If you are in Human Resources, this book gives new insight to into predicting who will succeed in sales positions and what special training your sales staff will need, based on whether they are selling Products, Services, or some combination of both.

Chapter Three

Is Your Definition of Services the Same as Your Definition of Pornography?

"I know it when I see it."

Supreme Court Justice Potter Stewart
on why he refused to provide a definition of pornography

What is the definition of a "Service"?

That question is something any businessperson should be able to answer… Right? Everybody knows what a Service is. We use them all the time.

I've found that, when pressed to give an answer, business managers respond in one of two ways:

1. Service as it relates to "customer service," exemplified by the statement, "This is a service industry… If the customer isn't getting good service, they can move to a competitor." These managers are concerned with answering the phone by the third ring, easy return policies, optimizing 24/7 operator availability, and so on.

2. Service as the company's offering, exemplified by the statement, "We provide XYZ to our customers," where XYZ is a clearly named Service, like legal representation, copywriting, or dry cleaning.

The title of this book promised a new science for marketing Services, so, for our purposes, we are interested in this latter definition, *Services as the primary business offering.*

Every science starts with basic definitions, so I'll come back to the question *What is a Service?*

Surely there must be a simple, operative definition of a Service—a definition that would allow us to immediately identify a Service offering, as opposed to a Product offering. Or, when Products and Services were offered jointly, we could easily identify the components.

For example, if I asked you to define a broom, you might answer that it's a cleaning tool made up of a handle with bristles at one end. The bristles facilitate pushing fine particles of dirt across a surface so they can be gathered and disposed of. The rule could be applied to any group of tools to quickly identify the brooms but also to keep from confusing them with "broom-shaped objects."

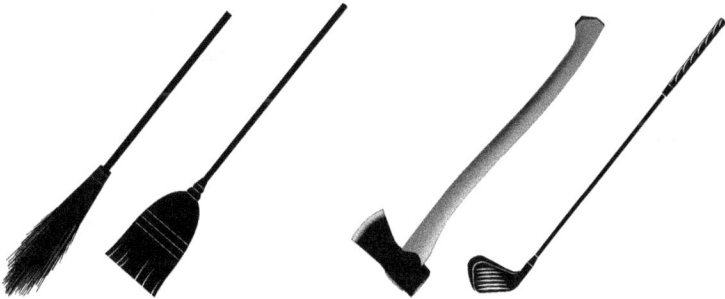

Brooms   Not Brooms

And yet....

I've "swept" firewood out of my way with my axe while I was chopping wood, so it might be suggested that an axe is a kind of broom. But if we use the operative definition, we can see that an axe is another kind of tool. It's not a cleaning tool, and it doesn't have bristles. It's a cutting tool, and although it has a handle, it doesn't have the bristles. Therefore, it's clearly not a broom, even though I used it for sweeping.

Between 1960 and 2000, there was no definition of Services that did not relate them to Products. It was a bit like defining cats this way: "You know when you're stroking a house pet, and it's not a dog, but it's furry like a dog, but it's not a dog, and it doesn't bark? That's a cat."

In 1960, the American Marketing Association defined a Service this way:

"Activities, benefits, or satisfactions which are offered for sale (or are provided) *in connection with the sale of goods"*

This definition suggests that Services are something offered as an *adjunct* to Products, and not a class of offering that is separate from manufactured goods. In other words, the AMA had no way of discussing healthcare, accountancy, design, project management, or cleaning services.

The first person to say essentially, "The emperor has no clothes" was Lynn Shostack, who was a VP at Citibank in 1977. Her seminal paper *Breaking Free From Product Marketing* insisted there were fundamental differences between tangible Products and intangible Services. In fact, it was this "intangibility" that she viewed as the key differentiator between Products and Services.

The last five marketing textbooks that I've taught from at The University of Winnipeg reference Shostack's work. Her work still defines the discussion more than 30 years later. Her paper begins,

"New concepts are necessary if service marketing is to succeed. Service marketing is an uncharted frontier. Despite the increasing dominance of services in the U.S. economy, basic texts still disagree on how services should be treated in a marketing context."

Does that argument sound familiar? Vargo, Lusch, Gummesson, and Lovelock said the same thing, but their quotes came three decades after Shostack raised the issue.

Shostack condemned the AMA for lumping Goods and Services into a single entity, and applying the term "intangible goods" for Services and Service-like offerings. As she puts it,

"It's a complete contradiction of terms. It is wrong to imply that services are just like products except for 'intangibility.' By such logic, apples are just like oranges, except for their 'apple-ness.' Intangibility isn't a modifier, it's a state."

Her arguments are summarized in her diagram "Scale of Market Entities," a list of Products and Services ordered according to how tangible they are.

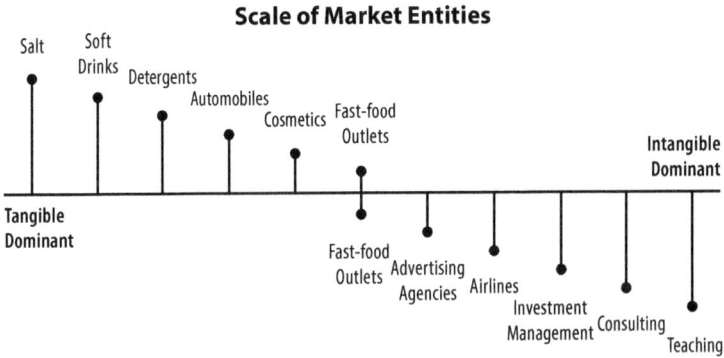

Scale of Market Entities

On the far left of her spectrum, at the Tangible Dominant side, is Salt. Salt is perfectly tangible. You know exactly what you're getting with salt, and with all five senses. Appears as a white, cubic, crystalline solid, hard and gritty to the touch, tastes salty, makes a crunching noise when rubbed between the fingers, and smells tangy. And the hidden, intangible aspect of salt is… nothing at all. If you are thinking of purchasing a box of salt, you can know exactly what you are getting ahead of time.

On the far right of her spectrum, at the Intangible Dominant side, is Teaching. The experience of being taught cannot be perceived before purchase. Even for students in the same class, the experience varies. One student may rate a teacher highly, another, poorly, even though they attended the same class. It's impossible to know what the outcomes will be before buying education. There is nothing tangible to take away from the experience or anything you could resell.

Along the spectrum come offerings that are not quite purely tangible or purely intangible. For example, dentistry is intangible dominant: The service is hard to imagine before it's received, but the patient may come away with a very tangible filling or crown. Cosmetics are tangible dominant: a buyer can pick up a lipstick—perhaps even try out a "tester"—but the benefits transcend a change of color. Part of the sales pitch for lipstick includes increased confidence, sex appeal, and peer acceptance.

The very middle of Shostack's spectrum includes fast-food outlets, what we would term today as quick-serve restaurants. She lists Fast Food twice, once as intangible dominant, and once as tangible dominant.

Do patrons at a restaurant buy a Product or a Service? Clearly, they're getting a Product. Whether it's rare filet mignon steak frites or a Big Mac with fries, the purchase is tangible: meat and potatoes, enhanced with the house's secret sauce.

At the same time, the high prices of a fine-dining establishment are based more on the level of service than the raw materials. The maître d' welcomes guests. The sommelier helps select a wine. Bus boys sweep away errant crumbs and keep water glasses filled.

Perhaps the waiter will prepare Cherries Jubilee at the table. The benefits of fine dining go beyond nutrition. There is the feeling of having been pampered, of being seen at the "right" establishment, and of enjoying food of a higher quality than could be had at home. This makes fine dining intangible dominant.

Fast food, on the other hand, lacks services. Patrons stand in line to order and carry their food themselves on trays to their tables. They fill their own soft drink cups at the fountain. At the end of the meal, they bus their trays to communal garbage cans.

The principal offering is clearly food, a tangible-dominant Product. Compare quick-serve food to a frozen TV-style dinner. Similar quality, pre-cooked, and then heated shortly before serving. The offering is tangible: Diners know exactly what they are getting before they order. McDonald's takes pride in the fact that you can buy a Big Mac anywhere and it will be exactly the same as one purchased anywhere else.

It would seem that fast food is more like a tangible Product than a Service.

And yet.

And yet.

The buyer didn't have to do the final cooking, or clean pans, or go to the grocery store. All of that was done, so there is clearly a Service component to fast food. That's why Shostack put it right in the middle of the tangible/intangible spectrum. In her mind, fast food was the point where Products and Services blurred into one another.

There's actually a simpler example, *The Vending Machine Problem*. I have two cans of Coke on my desk. The only difference between them is the price I paid, and in fact, I can no longer tell which is which. The can that was purchased at the grocery store cost 1/3 as much as the can purchased from a vending machine. Although the machine vended a purely tangible *Product,* the price I paid suggests that a *Service* of some kind was purchased without my being aware of it. Whatever it was that was worth the extra buck, it's not something I can easily see.

While Shostack's paper focused on the idea that *intangibility* was the defining characteristic that differentiated Products from Services, she also introduced the idea that Services were *ephemeral* processes that were experienced and rendered, and that *could not be stored or resold.*

Her observations formed the basis of what would be called the IHIP model, suggesting Services were Intangible, Heterogeneous (unique to each buyer), Inseparable (from the buyer), and Perishable. For the next three decades, this was the standard model of Services. Marketing practitioners and theoreticians used the IHIP as the basis for all further discussion. And for 30 years, nobody realized how wrong it was.

In the 1981 university-level textbook *Fundamentals of Marketing,* by William J. Stanton, the author explains, "Services are those separately identifiable, essentially intangible activities which provide want, satisfaction, and are not necessarily tied to the sale of a Product or another Service." In other words, *we can recognize Services because they are intangible.*

Not everybody agreed, though. That same year, in *The Harvard Business Review,* Theodore Levitt suggested that *all* Products and Services *have an element of intangibility.* He erroneously observed that "while services like insurance and transportation are nearly entirely intangible… so are goods… while they can be seen, they often cannot be tried out before they are purchased."

This would not be the last time it was suggested that Products and Services were essentially the same thing.

The IHIP model, sometimes called the "Four I's" model, proposed that Services could be differentiated from Products because Services had these four characteristics:

- Intangibility: Services don't have a physical form. You can't drop a Service on the floor. If I FedEx a package from NYC to LA, it's exactly the same when it gets there. You can't measure the package and say, "Aha! I've found the transportation I paid for." It's like the scientists who try to figure out how much a soul weighs by putting a dying patient on a scale.

- Inseparability: Services are closely tied to the buyer and can't be resold. If you do, it becomes a little surrealistic: My parents sent me for 12 years of piano lessons, but I don't really like to play. On the other hand, as a small business-man, I could really have a better understanding of finance. The other day, I met a retired accountant who had always wanted to play the piano. So we swapped. Now I understand how to calculate my payroll taxes, and he performs Saturday nights for tips at Jazzy's Lounge. It was bad timing, because I had just had my piano tuned but couldn't play anymore. Then I remembered my sister's piano needed tuning, so I gave the tuning to her.

- Inconsistency: Every time a Service is provided, it's a little bit different (or a *lot* different) from every other instance of that Service. Two students experience the same class, with the same teacher, but there is no consistency in what they take out of the classroom with them. With Products, *homogeneity* is a key measure of quality. With Services, *heterogeneity,* often in the form of customization, is the measure of quality. A teacher who can make material accessible to students with a variety of learning styles is praised for giving each student what they need to succeed.
- Inventory-less: Services are perishable. If a plane seat isn't filled at takeoff, then the value is lost forever. Services can't be inventoried for future use. A dentist can't make up for lost time when a patient misses an appointment by "doing some root canals" so they'll be ready to sell later.

By the mid-1990s, the IHIP model was integrated into most marketing textbooks that discussed Services as something separate from Products.

It would not be until 2004 that the model was widely challenged. Unfortunately, more than ten years after the publication of those challenges, 99% of all university marketing textbooks still teach the IHIP model.

Sadly, for those of us who were practitioners of sales and marketing, the IHIP model didn't offer very much useful advice. When the marketing team asked my opinion about illustrations for the new ad campaign, it didn't do my career any good to sagely point out that, since our company's consulting services were intangible, they should stop looking for pictures.

Think about it… What would they show? A group of people sitting in cubicles thinking hard about data? How would you show they were thinking hard? By drawing in little heat lines radiating off their heads?

Lynn Shostack felt that intangibility was the key differentiator of a Service and the key challenge of a Service business. Intangibility created a problem for purchasers in that they couldn't examine the offer before purchase. The marketing department can't put a picture of the service in the ad. The buyer couldn't "taste" a "sample" before deciding which provider to choose.

Products, on the other hand, are completely tangible. They have dimensions, weight, color, model numbers, SKUs. A Product can come in 31 fabulous flavors that you can see right there in the freezer case. Colored sprinkles or chocolate? Sugar cone or waffle cone? They're all right there on the counter for you to examine prior to purchase. You want to taste the caramel fudge ripple before you commit to a whole cone? There are special tiny spoons just for that purpose. The 31 flavors look delicious in the glossy magazine ad.

For the practitioners, working in marketing departments and ad agencies, intangibility was the key obstacle in advertising Services. There was no equivalent to the ice-cream rainbow in the Services world. For the auto-repair garage that selects from hundreds of sub-processes to create a unique solution that will restore a damaged car to its original state, the ad would have to be the size of a football field to fully describe all the processes available.

How readable is an ad like this? Explanatory, yes. Compelling, no.

Estimate: Our experienced estimators will inspect the damage, recoding and reporting all information using our computerized systems. This provides an estimate of the cost of repairs, although further hidden damage may be uncovered once the vehicle is disassembled.

Insurance Approval: Once the initial estimate is completed, we'll work with your insurance company to gain authorization to begin the repair process. We'll continue to communicate with the insurer over the course of repairs so there are no surprise costs to you.

Disassembly: Once the vehicle is disassembled, structural damage is determined along with other damage not visible during the initial estimating process. Your insurer will re-inspect the damage and re-approve the additional work, including additional parts that will have to be ordered.

Structural Repair: Structural repair returns the frame of your vehicle back to factory specifications. Quality of the work is assured using advanced measuring tools to monitor every stage of the work. Once the frame is restored, work can begin on the more visible parts of your vehicle.

Body Repair: Our body repair department will replace or repair damaged exterior panels. As new panels are installed and exposed metal parts refinished, the vehicle starts returning to its pre-accident appearance.

Paint: Our state-of-the-art downdraft paint booth uses the same technology and procedures as the factory. Primer insures solid paint adhesion, and clear coat layers ensure durability. We literally bake the shine onto your vehicle.

Reassembly: The vehicle is reassembled and details like modling and trim are put back on the vehicle. Final systems inspections take place, and any standard service repairs such as wheel alignment are completed.

Cleanup and Inspection: After we finish our work, we'll clean the vehicle inside and out, and have our inspectors check our repair team's work. We're not done until we're confident your vehicle is in pre-accident condition.

Completed: When we return your vehicle to you, we'll take the time to explain what was done and complete all your final insurance paperwork. You'll drive away knowing your vehicle is in the same condition as before your accident.

In my microcosm, the higher I got up the corporate ladder, the more I felt under the gun. Although my role was more direct business development, I kept getting called into meetings for the Marketing team. For some reason, the advertising specialists expected me—the head sales guy—to have answers to the questions they couldn't answer: How can our ads differentiate *our* consulting services from the consulting services of our competitors? How do we illustrate an offering that is best described as "many people thinking very hard about the client's business issues"? My CEO kept talking about "productizing" our services, whatever that meant.

I read voraciously: Technical papers, sales videos, blogs, always trying to stay ahead of the questions and always looking for advice that applied to Services. But inside my head, the conversation went like this:

Hey, Abbott! I don't know what graphics to run in the ads for my mechanical engineering firm.

Well, Costello, Why don't you show me a few pictures that sum up what you do? Maybe that will give us some ideas.

In the academic world, researchers were agreeing with the practitioners. In the mid-1980s, *The European Journal of Marketing, The Harvard Business Review,* and *Business Magazine* published articles like "Services Marketing—Managing the Intangibles," "Four Ways to Make Services More Tangible," and "Marketing Intangible Products and Product Intangibles." The best minds in the world were looking for ways to understand Services and make them as "advertise-able" as Products. And nobody had definitive answers.

Are you scoffing? Does it seem far-fetched that nobody in advertising understood how Services advertising had to differ from Product advertising, or that they didn't know what to put into ads for Services to make them effective?

Kathleen Mortimer is a researcher at the University of Northampton in the UK. The focus of her work is on the advertising of Services: how they differ from Product ads, what makes them effective, and how consumers shop online for Services. Especially intriguing are her investigations into whether or not the *theory* that is taught in business schools is congruent with *real-life activities* of practitioners. That is, if you showed an *Advertising Fundamentals* textbook to a 20-year veteran at a world-class ad agency, would the response be laughter or applause?

In 2001, the *Journal of Services Marketing* published the results of an experiment Mortimer conducted with creative directors at medium-sized advertising agencies. She specifically chose staff from firms that were big enough that the creative directors would have experience with a large variety of Products and Services, but not *so* big that they would be pigeonholed into a department that worked with clients from a single industry vertical.

Her study had three parts. First, she gave the participants a set of 18 cards, each of which had the name of a Product or a Service (e.g., insurance, jewelry). She asked them to sort the cards into groups "where the items had a common characteristic which would influence the creative approach." Once they completed the exercise, she reshuffled the cards and asked that they be divided as either Products or Services. Finally, she asked how their creative output for clients differed between Services and Products.

The results were interesting. Not one creative director naturally organized the cards by Products versus Services until prompted to do so. Their piles of cards had titles like "necessary evil," "distress purchases," and "tangible benefits." When given direction to make two piles, one for Services and one for Products, it became clear that they had no "standard" way of doing so. For example, one creative director identified a discount airline as being a Service (transportation) and another as a Product (because of the low level of service provided by a discount airline).

Two of the interviewees found the Product/Service classification "unhelpful and confusing." To quote from the study, their responses included:

"You might say Abby National [a credit union] is a Service, but it [an investment] is a Product because it's a clearly defined package—this is what I put in, and this is what I get out."

"A product is a service is a brand."

They also didn't see a problem with visualizing a Service. If needed, the graphics could show the service encounter, that is, the meeting of the buyer and provider, regardless of the nature of the service. Morton said, "The majority felt that showing the smiling female face of the service provider gave the organization a friendly and approachable image."

Her final conclusion was that advertising professionals aren't influenced by whether the ad they are creating is a Product or a Service, and that "some have difficulty differentiating between the two."

No wonder I was feeling so stupid. Everybody in the industry was behaving like we had all the answers, even though our level of understanding was so low that we didn't even have a clear cut definition of Services. There was no body of "best practices" to advise managers of Service businesses. And yet nobody was suggesting that there was anything wrong with the situation.

And then in 2006, everything changed.

Chapter Four

Defining the Undefinable

At the dawn of the 21st century, the business world had a very limited definition of Services. As a "definition," IHIP defined the problems and limitations of discussing Services marketing, but it didn't give advice to managers that could guide their decisions. Its only redeeming facet was that it at least gave a framework for asking more questions.

As somebody with a budget to meet, "more questions" wasn't exactly what I was looking for.

In 2004, two parallel journals published two similarly themed papers.

The first, entitled "Whither Services Marketing—In Search of a New Paradigm and Fresh Perspectives," pointed out that the IHIP "framework has serious weaknesses" and called for a new paradigm that would offer "a reanalysis of extant but unused knowledge."[1] The authors, Dr. Christopher Lovelock and Dr. Evert Gummesson, respectively professors at Yale University and Stockholm University, systematically picked apart the IHIP model, and offered a suggestion about what might take its place.

The first 22 pages are dedicated to a history of the problem. Only 2½ pages are devoted to their thesis. They suggested that the key attribute that defined "Services" was the concept of ownership versus non-ownership. Put simply, *you can own a Product, but you can't own a Service.* The rest of the paper pays its respects to existing theories, while offering contradictory examples. First the "I," then the "H," then the other "I," then the "P." One after the other, each cornerstone is attacked.

The second paper is titled "Four Service Marketing Myths." These authors, Dr. Steven Vargo and Dr. Robert Lusch[2], pulled no punches about how they felt about the IHIP model, as can be seen in the subtitle of their paper: "Remnants of a Goods-Based Manufacturing Model." They state clearly that IHIP characteristics "do not distinguish Services from goods" and that the IHIP characteristics "only have meaning from a manufacturer's perspective."

Their model considers Services to be at the core of all value creation and advocates switching to a Services-as-the-norm model. They argue that a taxi provides the same Service (transportation)

---

[1] Sorry. That's how academics talk.
[2] Dr. Vargo is "only" a visiting professor at the R.H. School of Business, University of Maryland, but he has 20 years' C-suite experience as a marketing practitioner and has published numerous peer-reviewed journals. Dr. Lusch is Dean of the M.J. Neeley School of Business. His publications include more than 150 peer-reviewed articles and 16 books. He has also served as Chair of The American Marketing Association.

as a car, but that the car provides the Service in a "tangible product" manner. They call this outlook <u>S</u>ervice <u>D</u>ominant <u>L</u>ogic, or S-D Logic for short. To arrive at their conclusions, they also chop away at the IHIP convention, offering numerous counter-examples and pointing out inconsistencies.

I had always accepted the IHIP model as correct, even though I found it unhelpful in making business decisions. Now some of the best minds studying business theory were also saying it was incorrect.

That's a pretty big paradigm shift. Could it be correct? Could it be there were flaws in the IHIP model?

I presented the question to my students in the *Introduction to Marketing* course I taught at The University of Winnipeg. First, I delivered the IHIP model as was covered in the textbook. Then I told them it was an old approach and could be wrong. Finally I asked them simply, "Can you spot any flaws?"

Bang! Kaboom! Of all the questions I've asked classes, this was the only one where *every* hand shot up. Everybody had a complaint about IHIP. Some of the things I heard:

- Intangible Products:
  - The CPU in my laptop has 1,303,000,000 transistors. I have no way of understanding how many that is. The salesman said it was a lot. Is it enough? I have no way to get my head around that. And what's a transistor, anyway?
  - The CPU is running at 3.8 gigahertz[3].

---

[3] If you say so. My stopwatch measures down to only a 10th of a second.

- Honda Civic ad brags it has a CVTEC engine. But it still burns gas[4], right?
- Tangible Services:
  - Wash-dry-fold at the local laundromat. I take in a crumpled heap of dirty clothes and take away folded clean clothes. I can picture that exactly.
  - I rented a hotel room. I knew exactly what I was getting before I checked in.
- Enduring Services:
  - My house is *still* painted.
  - I'm hoping to remember what I learned when I leave university.
- Ephemeral Products:
  - Candy
  - There's an expression about this: You can't have your cake and eat it, too. It means if you eat your cake, it's gone. Cake is ephemeral[5].
- Separable Services:
  - A stamp (transportation) is good on any envelope up to a certain weight.
  - A gift certificate for a massage.
  - Banking is a huge network that exists long before I open an account or take out a mortgage.
- Inconsistent Products:

---

[4] I think car companies have a lot of gall to brag that their engines are "the most advanced." 150 years after the invention of the modern internal combustion engine, more than 99% of the cars on the road are still powered by the liquefied remains of dead dinosaurs.

[5] Assuming we are successful in avoiding the inevitable scatological jokes

- Subway sandwiches—Made to order, but completely tangible.

I was reminded of the expression, "Out of the mouths of babes come gems." These were first- and second-year Business students. They hadn't read hundreds of papers that took IHIP as gospel. Given the permission to do so, they immediately tore apart the prevailing theory discussed in our textbook. In some cases, they recreated examples given by Vargo, Lusch, Lovelock, and Gummesson[6].

Well if IHIP is wrong… What are Services?

Vargo and Lusch say "Everything's a Service." Lovelock and Gummesson say it's a Service if it can't be owned. There were many other suggestions. My favorite was that Service providers were in a symbiotic relationship with Service purchasers, similar to that between remoras and sharks, with each contributing something to the relationship.

The Journal of Production and Operations Management is one of *Business Week Magazine*'s premier journals. That means when *Business Week* ranks MBA programs at business schools, it uses publication in *JPOM* as an indicator of quality.

In 2006, *JPOM* published the missing link for understanding the true nature of Services: "Foundations and Implications of a Proposed Unified Services Theory." The paper used the term "unified" to indicate that the theory would apply to any Service, past, present, or future, B2B or B2C, large or small.

---

[6] I've been careful to never repeat this exercise with any other theory. Who knows what other fields of study they might destroy?

Co-written by Scott Sampson and Craig Froehle, it introduced a new and robust operative definition of "Services" that, at the same time, provided a contrasting definition of "Products."

Dr. Scott Sampson is a Professor of Business and Services Operations Management at Brigham Young University's Marriott School of Management[7]. His recent award-winning papers include "What Are Services? An Empirical Investigation" and "Why We Need an Operations Service Paradigm." He also won the IBM Faculty Award[8] for being a leader in the field of Service operations.

Dr. Froehle is a professor instructing at The University of Cincinnati in *both* the Linder College of Business *and* at University of Cincinnati's College of Medicine. He's a leading expert in Service operations at healthcare facilities, with an interesting set of credentials that include a BSc in Mechanical Engineering, an MBA, a PhD in Operations Management, and founding and selling an online data-management company during the dot. com boom.

Unified Services Theory (UST) defines and contrasts Products and Services. For convention's sake[9], we'll look at the definition of Product first.

According to UST, a Product is anything that can be made without input from the end consumer, except for *final selection* and *payment.*

---

[7] Longest job title ever?
[8] With its $40,000 prize
[9] Nobody ever says "Services and Products." It's always "Products and Services."

For example: I walk into a store, and I see an array of shirts on the shelves. I choose the red-shirt-in-size-large and pay. My only input into the Production of the shirt is final selection and payment.

On the other hand, UST says that a Service requires an additional kind of input besides selection and payment: It requires one of three kinds of *Service Inputs*. Specifically, these inputs can be the customer's *property,* the customer's *information,* or the customer's *person.* That is:

- My dry cleaner cannot clean my *suit* until I drop it off.
- My accountant cannot prepare my taxes until I provide my *T-slips.*
- My dentist can't fill my *cavities* until I personally sit in the chair.

Formally, UST is stated as follows:

"With service processes, the customer provides significant inputs into the production process. With manufacturing processes, groups of customers may contribute ideas to the design of the product, but individual customers' only participation is to select and consume the output. All managerial themes unique to services are founded in this distinction."

Note that the definition uses the term "customer," singular, and not "customers," plural. The theory differentiates between groups of potential buyers that provide input to the manufacturing process (aka market research) and an individual buyer's Service Inputs (SI). Market research is good input, but it's not required to manufacture a Product[10].

UST is more than just a definition to me. It's a tool for understanding complex offerings. It's a scalpel to dissect and a microscope to zoom in with.

This book started questioning the difference between a store-bought suit and a bespoke suit.

Does a tailor offer a Product or a Service? Easy to know with UST!

The work the tailor does is a Service. Martino can't begin making me a suit until I choose my fabric. I also have to provide my measurements and my preferences regarding style, number of pockets, vents, width of lapel, final selection of fabric, and so on.

The fabric is a Product. The only input Martino and I provide to the fabric manufacturer is choice of fabric and payment. At that point, I own the fabric. Martino has my measurements on file but needs me there again after the fabric is cut to start finishing it to my body. The service inputs I provide to Martino are my property (cloth), my information (measurements), and my person (from neck to ankles).

And the "manufactured" off-the-rack suit? The cloth is a Product that the suit manufacturer buys. The manufacturer owns the fabric, and it's an input into their process. The manufacturer makes thousands of suits in a variety of popular styles and colors

---

[10] A manufacturer may decide to spend money producing chocolate-garlic-licorice ice cream but will find after the fact that consumers do not *select* it or *pay* for it.

in the hopes that somebody will want to buy them. Those suits are Products. I choose one and make my payment. After the suit becomes my property, I can take my suit to a tailor and purchase tailoring services to make my suit fit me better. In this case, the service inputs are my property (the suit) and my information (measurements).

Why do I think that Sampson and Froehle's UST is so much more valuable than the many new models defining Services, such as the ones discussed earlier in this chapter?

While the others are all well-thought-out ways of organizing and considering the characteristics of Products and Services, only UST gives me a clear, operative definition to tell them apart. In fact, some theories, like SD-Logic, blur the differences between them.

The confirmation for UST comes in its ability to encompass and explain all the other theories.

- Do you identify with Vargo and Lusch's take on Service's place in economic theory? Then UST lets you identify all the Service sub-processes that make up manufacturing.
- Do you like Lovelock and Gummesson's idea that Products and Services are differentiated by ownership and that Services aren't "owned"? Then UST explains that the Service is added to the original ownership of the service inputs that were provided by the buyer. (The tailor hemmed my new off-the-rack suit. The Service became part of what had originally been my property. I paid for the tailoring, and I "own" the Service because it's been incorporated into "my" suit.)

- UST explains that buying a stamp or a gift certificate for a massage isn't a Service transaction because the buyer did not provide Service Inputs. The stamp and gift certificate are forms of currency that *any* buyer could use to purchase services by providing SI in the form of property (letter to mail) or person (sore back and shoulder).

Unified Services Theory explains the phenomenon of The Four I's:

- Inseparable? Of course, because the Service doesn't occur until the buyer provides his or her own service inputs, and the value of the Service is now tied to the buyer's property. That's why a freshly painted house is worth more than one that needs painting. If I sell the house with its fresh coat of paint, the new owner gets that paint job. That's why a house that is "fixed up" is worth more than a "fixer upper."
- Inconsistent? Of course. Because each buyer provides different service inputs, the resulting outputs are also unique.
- Inventory-less? Of course, because the Service can't be started until the buyer provides service inputs. Ephemeral? It only seems that way because the Service becomes tied to the tangible service inputs. While it's true that, when the process of "doing my taxes" is done, the tax return endures, and the value of the Service endures with it.
- And the fourth, big, I? Intangible? UST lets us take apart that fallacy, and, as we'll see in the next chapter, provides a road map to productize any Service.

The other thing I like about UST is its simplicity. There's a certain "Duh Factor." Once you've heard UST, it's hard to understand why it wasn't stated 60 years earlier. In fact, in writing this book, I knew I'd have to give some history for readers to understand why it was so profound.

My first degree is in the sciences. High school biology students learn the difference between mammals and other kinds of animals. Mammals have hair and make milk for their young. To identify a mammal, just answer the question, "Does it have hair and milk?" If the answer is yes, it's a mammal. Any exceptions? Nope. Are bats the world's ugliest bird, or some kind of hideous gigantic bug? Bats have fur, and the mommy bats feed their baby bats bat-milk from bat-breasts. They're mammals, just like we are. Are dolphins mammals or just big smart fish? You get the picture.

In the same way that the science of biology gives clear-cut operational definitions of mammals and other kinds of animals, Unified Services Theory defines the differences between Products and Services.

And that definition makes a logical—even a scientific—study of Services possible.

And that's where this book comes in. The next chapters take the existing body of theories and best practices as they apply to Sales and Marketing, and apply UST to refine them.

How to Shoot Your Mouth Off, Without Shooting Yourself in the Foot

nified Services Theory is a new approach that completely contradicts the accepted canon of business theory about Services. As a first-time business author, it was a bit nerve wracking to find myself discussing a theory that A) nobody had ever heard of, and B) questioned the basic assumptions currently taught in business-school classrooms around the world.

In self-defense[1], I made a point of discussing UST as often as possible to anybody who would listen: colleagues at the university, junior salespeople selling landscaping door-to-door, trusted friends working in a multitude of Service industries, especially the ones working in marketing-related services, such as advertising, PR,

---

[1] It seems much of what I do is in self-defense.

or market research. I wanted to make sure that the book I was writing wasn't going to be a career-ender[2].

It was great practice fielding their challenges to UST. Their numerous, numerous challenges. Fortunately, I realized that most of these challenges were based on (alleged) exceptions to UST such as;

- My ad agency provides me with creative Products, finished ads that I own.
- Car rental "Services." Duh. I'm getting a car. That's a Product.
- Restaurants of every kind. Everybody brings up restaurants, especially McDonald's. This brings us right back to Lynn Shostack.
- The suit manufacturer has hundreds of tailors using special equipment that lets them make thousands of suits at once. Martino's Men's Fashion has just one Martino, and he has just one sewing machine, and can sew just one suit at a time. Both are manufacturing suits. It's a question of scale, not genre.
- Syndicated market research studies[3]. Market research is recognized as a Service, but syndicated reports appeared to be a "market research Product" that didn't require service inputs prior to production. It also had a set price, set

---

[2] I very much enjoyed your book, Mr. Selch. *Service Reboot* was one of the funniest things I've ever read. I'm pleased to tell you the leadership at McKinsey and Company is prepared to offer you an internship on our janitorial staff.

[3] If you aren't familiar with syndicated market research studies, these are market research projects that are researched and written "on spec" in the hopes that many companies will want to buy them. You are probably familiar with JD Power's automotive studies, or the University of Michigan's Confidence Index, but there are thousands of others with very narrow focus.

dimensions (245 pages) and could be previewed prior to purchase like any other Product.

- Steam-cleaning services: We'll clean any three rooms in your home for $99. I know what I'm getting, and it has a set price. I can even click a button on their website to purchase. That sounds like a Product.
- I can book a massage and pre-pay for it, and the therapist doesn't care who shows up for the appointment. Product, right?

The point that everybody was making[4] can be summarized this way: It seems that there are Services that behave like Products and Products that behave like Services.

This is actually a boon, rather than a problem, because it brings us to one of the first lessons implied by UST: A one-step process that lets you productize any Service. Let's examine that issue more closely.

It's harder to advertise a Service than a Product, for all the reasons mentioned in Chapter One. For decades, marketers have looked for ways to productize a Service. That is, to make a Service into something that can be promoted in the same way as Products, and purchased just as easily.

The dream was simple: Wouldn't it be nice if a professional offering interior decorating (or social work or editing) could put a "click to buy" button on their website[5]?

---

[4] ...and perhaps you are yourself as you read this book...

[5] I'll take a pound of corned beef, small tub of coleslaw, and, uh, oh yeah, coordinate the support services offered by agencies in my area to help my aging mother live independently and not have to go into a nursing home. And six of the big pickles, please.

The hope was that by productizing the offering, the provider could make the intangible tangible and make their Service as easy to buy as a bag of M&Ms.

The idea wasn't new. In 1989, *The European Journal of Marketing* published "The Marketing of Services: Managing the Intangibles."[6] The authors, who represented both worlds—marketing practitioners and marketing academics—summarized the problem with this quote:

"We haven't got anything to show customers like a can of baked beans."

Of course, many Services result in tangible outcomes. An engineering firm can show pictures of the bridges and museums it has designed, but the danger is that the next customer will say something like, "Well, our university is building a new complex to house our growing Faculty of Life Sciences. All you're showing us are pictures of bridges and museums and shopping malls. We were really hoping to find a company with the right kind of experience."[7]

Even at a smaller scale, there's no guarantee that showing pictures of "past best work" will be a driver of purchase for future clients. My mother's friend decorated her house with the help of a top interior designer. It was beautifully executed and exactly represented the friend's taste. My mother's response to the new décor could be summarized as "Yikes." She said she couldn't see

---

[6] By Angela M. Rushton of the firm Marketing Matters and David J. Carson of the Marketing Department at University of Ulster

[7] This scenario is based on an actual conversation I had with a client.

how the designer stayed in business by "turning a really nice home into a monstrosity."

The question of Service Productization continues, and Googling the subject will uncover many consultants specializing in this area.

What does UST have to say about productization? What can be learned from the paradox of "Services that behave like Products, and Products that behave like Services"?

If it is actually the case that these misbehaving Products and Services exist, then we can identify four categories:

- Products
- Services
- Service-y Products—that is, Products that behave like Services
- Product-y Services—that is, Services that behave like Products

Let's take a closer look to better understand these last two new categories, starting with an example of a Service-y Product:

Rauland-Borg is a very successful hardware manufacturer. They "design and build high-reliability solutions for healthcare facilities, schools, and other institutions." If you've been in a hospital, you know their products, even if you don't know their company name. You know the little button-on-a-cord that a patient clicks to call for a nurse? Rauland-Borg makes that button.[8]

---

[8] Also the incredibly complex network of behind-the-scenes infrastructure that makes sure when you need a nurse you can damn well call a nurse, with 100% uptime, no excuses. You can insert your own hospital horror story here, but really, when you need help from a nurse, Rauland-Borg is in the business of calling one for you.

But there's no e-store on the Rauland-Borg website to order their products. You can't just click-to-buy one ACC1110 Recessed-mount, round, corrosion-resistant, welded 22-guage steel backbox, no matter how badly you would like to have its rust-retardant exterior finish and heavily undercoated interior that eliminates mechanical resonances. Even though you can't buy it, it's still a Product, because if they wanted to sell it to you, all they would need from you would be final selection and payment.

There seems to be an assumption with Rauland-Borg's products that they will be sold accompanied by expertise-based services of some kind. In fact, the brochure for the ACC1110 is hidden behind a customer login gateway, and the brochure has a dedicated section that helps architects and engineers (Service providers) specify the part in *their* quotations and blueprints.[9]

That's because Rauland-Borg sells its products within the context of a "healthcare communications solution." When a hospital is being built, Rauland's global network of installers work with the hospital directors to design and install a communications network that will integrate with the hospital's IT and patient-care systems. Every installation is different, with Rauland-Borg's installers offering expertise to the architects and medical staff that will take the hospital from the blueprint stage to the "filled with patients" stage.

To create the plan, Rauland's installers need to know everything about the hospital… how many patient rooms and nursing

---

[9] I didn't hack my way in to the customer area. I found the brochure first by Googling for a Rauland-Borg brochure and then saw from the URL that it was sitting behind a login gateway called "Customer Connection," which provides access for distributors, customers, and R-B staff.

stations, floor layout, what other brands of equipment will be used, and a hundred other details.

Does that sound familiar? It's starting to sound like what UST would call Service Input, in this case, the customer's information.

Unified Services Theory lets us identify Rauland-Borg's hardware as a Product. It is designed and made in advance, without inputs from individual buyers. The only inputs they need from their customers are final selection and payment.

The installers are offering a series of services, the most obvious of which is installing the hardware in the hospital. But they also offer expertise in system design. Here are two of Rauland-Borg's U.S. distributors. Look at how they describe their operations on their websites:

- *ASCC is a full-service information technology company and network integration company. Our mission is to develop cost-effective, standards-compliant solutions for your network problems... We handle all aspects of the installation, from structured wiring through software configuration.*

- *Ronco Specialized Systems is a system integrator... supplies and services custom educational, commercial, and healthcare communication systems... and the best engineered solutions. We are one of the largest Rauland-Borg distributors in the country.*

Look at all the verbs: *integrate, develop, install, service, supply, engineer, distribute.* Ronco and ASCC are Service companies that sell Rauland-Borg (and other manufacturers') products.

The manufacturers they represent rely on them to answer questions like: How many of each type of connector? What is the least expensive configuration of R-B equipment? When during hospital construction should each piece of R-B equipment be installed? How can we ensure that the new R-B equipment integrates with legacy equipment? UST tells us these are all Services, because they require information (service inputs) from the customer before the consulting services can begin.

It's clear, though, that Rauland-Borg produces Products. I can hold that ACC1110 backbox in my hand, drop it on the floor, or spray-paint it purple, just like I could an apple or a chair. It has features and benefits that I can compare to competing Products. But it's always sold *coupled to Services,* so it's a kind of "Service-y Product."

Here's another, simpler, example of a Service-y Product: car rental. They say it's a Service, but clearly what I'm getting is a car. If I buy a car and sell it two days later, it's still me buying a Product. Shortening the length of time I own the car does not change the nature of a car from "Product" to "Service." How does that differ from me getting my car-Product from a "Service" agency for the same two-day period?

A hint to the solution is found in the NAICS code[10] for a car-rental agency: 53211. All industries starting with the prefix 53 are

---

[10] The North American Industrial Classification System (NAICS) uses a series of code numbers to classify businesses. The first digits identify the major vertical, and the last four break out the sub-industries. Similar businesses should have similar NAICS codes. For example, 53 refers to the Real Estate, Rentals, and Leasing. 532 is rentals and leasing. 53211 specifies the rental and leasing of auto equipment. Short-term car rentals is 532111, 532120 is rental of trucks and RVs, 532210 is consumer appliance rental, and 532220 is formal wear and costume rental.

defined in NAICS as follows: *Establishments that provide a wide array of tangible goods, such as automobiles, computers, consumer goods, and industrial machinery and equipment, to customers in exchange for a periodic rental or lease payment.*

To paraphrase: Rental agencies provide services that facilitate the short-term use of an object without requiring the long-term ownership of the object.

What are the service inputs? Specific times, specific locations, identity and age of buyer, how many passengers, etc.

If it's not clear to you that "when" is valid as a Service Input, imagine calling any national car rental agency and asking to reserve a car, but explaining you have no idea when you'll need it, where you want to pick it up, or who will be driving.[11]

These two examples (hospital communications equipment and cars that are rented rather than purchased) are examples of Products that masquerade as Services.

Going the other way, it's easier to spot Services that behave like Products. For example, we can differentiate between a carpet-cleaning *Service* and a carpet-cleaning *Product-y Service.*

Carpet cleaning *Service:* Our estimators will come to your location, measure the area, and provide a quotation based on the size and amount of dirt. That's a regular Service. Vendors can't add value until they gain access to my carpet, and they can't even quote a price until they get some information about my carpet. Writing a quote requires Service Input, and gathering that input is part of the estimation process.

---

[11] Sounds like an episode of *Seinfeld.*

Carpet cleaning *Product-y Service:* We'll steam clean any three rooms in your home for $99. Heavy dirt pre-removal, Scotch-guarding, spot stain removal available at additional cost.

Regardless of how it's offered, carpet cleaning is always a Service; the provider can't add value until they receive Service Input, in this case the dirty carpet. However, the offer to clean the carpet can be made one of two ways.

- By providing a specific quotation based on the buyer's exact situation. That kind of quote requires service inputs (information about the carpets to be cleaned) before an offer can be made.

- By providing a quotation based on certain assumptions about the "average" buyer. When the vendor says "clean any three rooms for $99," they are assuming the buyer doesn't live in Buckingham Palace, and "three rooms" means around 800 square feet or so.

Here's another example contrasting Services and Product-y Services:

Market research *Service:* Provide us with details of your business issues, and we'll provide a proposal for a research project that will inform your business decisions. The costs of recent ad hoc projects have ranged from a few thousand dollars to a few hundred thousand dollars.

Market research *Product-y Service*[12] (Let me quote from the website of an international firm):

> In general, we use a rule of thumb that we charge our regular clients $7500 per focus group, with a focus group defined as: A group session investigating issues concerning a consumer brand, product, or political issue held at a professional focus group facility in a major U.S. population center. We will recruit and compensate at least 8 participants between the ages of 18 and 60 who are able to answer questions about general consumer issues. Price includes a RIVA-certified professional moderator, two hours of pre-group meetings with the client, transcripts of session verbatims, and a report of findings. Coffee and Danish will be served as refreshments for clients wishing to observe the groups in person. Any deviation requires re-pricing.

There are similarities between a Product and a Product-y Service (e.g., set-price carpet cleaning):

- *Both* are offered
    - with a set price
    - with easily envisioned specifications and descriptions (tangible)
    - without requiring service inputs

---

[12] We've discussed three kinds of offerings in the market research industry. The syndicated study explained earlier in this chapter was a market research Product that was researched, written, and published in the hopes that somebody would select it and pay for it. The focus group is an example of what we are now calling a Product-y Service. The core Service on which they are based is the ad hoc, bespoke, research project undertaken to answer the client's specific business question.

There are similarities between a Service and a Service-y Product (e.g., hospital communications equipment):

- *Neither* can be offered
  - with a set price
  - with easily envisioned specifications and descriptions (intangible)
  - without requiring service inputs

In the case of the Product-y Service, SI is still needed to *fulfill* the Service, but those service inputs are not needed to *sell* the Services. That is, regardless of how the price quote is calculated, the carpet cleaner still needs to access the carpet in order to clean it. The service input of carpet is required. Therefore, it's always a Service.

When a Service can be sold without first receiving Service Input, it can be sold like a Product. When an offering requires service inputs in order just to make the sale, then it needs to be sold like a Service.

I understand these hyphenated-y terms are cumbersome, and I'll give them better names a few pages from now. I use the terms at this point to underscore that the fundamental nature of the Product and Service don't change just because they are modified to be sold like their opposite counterpart.

Therefore, converting a Service into a Product is simply a matter of removing the variability from the pre-sale service inputs.

The conversion of a Service to a Product is a one-step process:

Step One: Define and constrain the service inputs[13]

Here is a simple example: Dry cleaning, as a Service, varies in cost and complexity, depending on the articles being cleaned. Down comforters or parkas will take far longer to dry than handkerchiefs. A handmade quilt pieced together from antique silk remnants will need far more attention than a white cotton dress shirt with ring-around-the collar. Even pressing a pleated skirt requires discussion. 10 pleats or 100 pleats?

To give a price quote, the dry cleaner needs to know what service inputs will be provided by the customer: fabric, size of item, degree of soil, final preparations (Hanger? Box? Stainproofing?), and timeframe (rush or regular processing).

To productize the cleaning Service into an offering that can be sold as a Product, the cleaner *defines* and *constrains* the service inputs:

- Any cotton or cotton-blend dress shirt dry cleaned, pressed, and hung for $1.99. Two-day turnaround. Folded and boxed $1 extra. Stain removal, if needed, $1 extra.

Fabric—cotton or cotton blend; Size—fits a human; Degree of Soil—unstained; Final Preparations—Hanger; Timeframe—two days. *When the service inputs are defined and constrained, a set price can be given—$1.99*

---

[13] That's the whole process. There is no step two.

Can that process be scaled to a more complicated business, like creative B2B advertising services? Would the "define and constrain" approach work with an IT firm or a Marketing consultancy?

Let's try all three at once: Imagine an IT marketing consulting company that specializes in website development. When they sit down with a client to discuss their creative and technical offerings, the sky is the limit. It's a perfect Service: The provider can't begin the project before receiving Service Input, and there's no way to estimate the price without knowing what form the site will need to take. Will it be five pages, or fifty? Embedded videos linked to order forms, or just text and still pictures? Content updated daily or annually? How much client facetime is needed? How much reporting? How much strategic guidance? What other services (SEO, ecommerce, etc.) are needed? What industry? High fashion or farmers' cooperative?

Can an offering as complex as *marketing* or *website development* be productized so a prospective customer can "click here" to purchase?

TourismTiger.com is a company that has successfully productized their B2B ecommerce website design service by essentially implementing the one-step process:

○ TourismTiger creates websites for tour operators, leveraging their technical and industry expertise to create websites that drive more bookings for tour operators.

○ These websites are based on a proven 12-page model: Home, About, Contact, FAQ, Privacy, Bookings, Blog, and up to five pages unique to the customer.

- ○ Content updates are done as the client provides new content, but the basic structure (12 pages) is based on their proven system, which leverages the fact that 45% of all bookings are done on mobile devices.
- ○ No deviations: Email by Google Apps; Integration with all industry-standard tourism booking software system (but nothing else such as Salesforce); Google Analytics and Google SEO.
- ○ Seven-day turnaround. Price is $499 plus $59/month. Cancel anytime.
- • Client is expected to provide content (information and photos)

Everything in the above list with a white circle is a Service Input that has been defined and constrained by TourismTiger. com. By productizing their Service, they can sell it the same way any other Product is sold. The black dot signifies the input that is needed to actually provide the service of building the customer's website, after the service is sold.[14]

The define-and-constrain method does scale to complex intellectual-property-heavy services, just as well as it does to a mixing a latte. Because Unified Services Theory applies to *all* Services, observations and conclusions based on UST are also universally applicable.

---

[14] Shortly before publication of this book, TourismTiger moved to a pure Service model and no longer offers their productized service. Their original websites can be viewed using Internet Archive's Wayback Machine: http://archive.org/web/.

We can now go back to Lynn Shostack's original Product/
Service continuum and re-assign each of its offerings into one
of four categories: Products, Services, Product-y Services, and
Service-y Products.

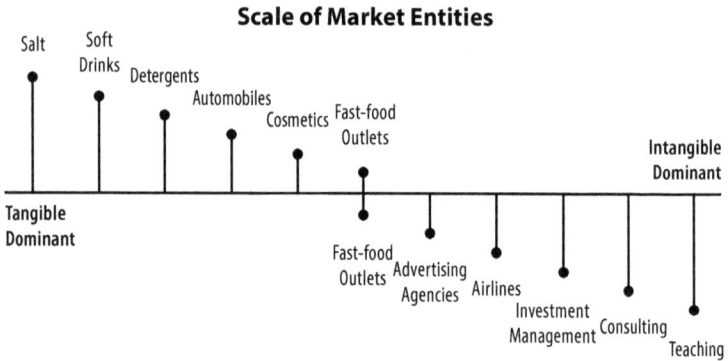

Scale of Market Entities

Salt Soft
      Drinks Detergents
                     Automobiles
                          Cosmetics Fast-food
                                     Outlets

Tangible
Dominant

Intangible
Dominant

Fast-food
Outlets Advertising
         Agencies Airlines
                        Investment
                        Management Consulting
                                    Teaching

Products: salt, soft drinks, detergents, automobiles, cosmetics

Services: teaching, consulting, investment management,
advertising agencies

Product-y Services: airline seats—The ticket has a set price
based on its characteristics (e.g., business class on the 5:10 am
flight from Boston to Chicago). The buyer makes final selection
of a seat on a plane based on those characteristics. No passenger
inputs are needed for the airline to make the offer. Service inputs in
the form of the passenger's body are needed to provide the service.

Service-y Product: fast food outlets—The burger is always the
same. No service inputs are needed to produce burgers. However,
buyers must provide information about *when* they want to eat,
and the food is prepared at that time. In fact, the modern term

for the category is "quick serve" because the Service that is tied to the Product is to prepare it quickly when ordered[15].

We've applied Unified Services Theory to solve Shostack's 40-year-old conundrum.

As we go into the next chapter, remember:

Products and Product-y Services are sold like Products. (Final selection and payment only)

Services and Service-y Products are sold like Services. (Selection, payment, and service inputs)

---

[15] Burger King differentiated themselves from McDonald's by promoting their willingness to customize the burger as it was being made. In essence, they asked for additional service inputs regarding the customer's preferences.

Chapter Five

The Fix Is In

Stripped of complications, a sale can be defined as an exchange of value between two parties. The value can be represented by money, products, services, or any combination. I can pay cash for a candy bar or a foot massage; Russian grain has been exchanged for Iranian oil.

There are proxies that allow a sale to be "made" prior to the physical exchange, such as a contract signing, but these are just proxies, guaranteeing the approval and intent of the parties to make the exchange.

We could paraphrase the Unified Services Theory's definitions of Products and Services this way:

For a sale to occur (that is, for there to be an exchange of value) there is a difference between what a Product buyer must provide to the seller and what a Service buyer must provide. The Product buyer must provide final selection and payment for the Product. The Service buyer selects the Service and pays for it but must also provide service inputs. Until the service inputs are provided, there can be no exchange of value.[1]

I think it's really interesting that UST's definition of "Service" calls attention to *when* the provider adds value for the buyer. In the case of Products, it's before the sales transaction, and in the case of Services, it's after the sales transaction.

In fact, I would suggest an equally good differentiator between Products and Services is that Services are offerings where the vendor adds value *after* the sale, and Products have value added *before* the sale.[2]

Focus on that for a moment. The difference between a Product and a Service is whether the vendor adds value before or after the sale. Intuitively, we should suspect that the *sales process* will somehow be different between Products and Services.

On the following page are simplified diagrams for the two processes.[3]

Take a close look at the two diagrams. The path for selling Services is not the same as the path for selling Products. Did you catch that? *Unified Services Theory implies that the process of selling Services has fundamentally different requirements than selling Products.*

---

[1] This, of course, applies only to "regular services," not "product-y services." For the balance of this book, unless otherwise stated, we will be considering "regular" Services that require SI to be sold.

[2] Car dealerships sell and service cars. Every aspect of the car's features and benefits are added during design and manufacture, before the sale. After the sale, the car company adds value with its Service department. That's why the two big divisions at any dealership are Sales and Service.

[3] Simplified to the point of being incorrect. In the next chapter, we'll look at a few more accurate and more useful diagrams.

**Product
Sales Path**

**Simplified Service
Sales Path**

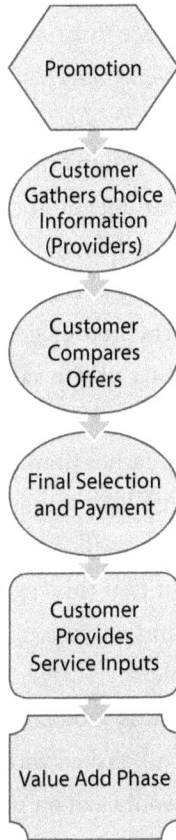

```
Value Add Phase

   ↓

 Promotion                    Promotion

   ↓                            ↓

Customer                     Customer
Gathers Choice               Gathers Choice
Information                   Information
(Products)                   (Providers)

   ↓                            ↓

Customer                     Customer
Compares                     Compares
Offers                       Offers

   ↓                            ↓

Final Selection              Final Selection
and Payment                  and Payment

                                ↓

                             Customer
                             Provides
                             Service Inputs

                                ↓

                             Value Add Phase
```

LEGEND

⬡ Advertising/Promotion/
Selling Phase

⬭ Purchasing Process Phases

▭ Service Inputs Phases

▢ Company Creates Value

My career can be summarized as 25 years selling and marketing Services and "Intangible Products." I've been to seminars, read books, and moved up the company ladder discussing corporate marketing challenges with people more experienced and smarter than myself.

UST was the first time that anybody suggested that selling (marketing/promoting/advertising) a Service was fundamentally different from selling a Product.

Brian Tracy didn't mention it. There's was nothing in my Miller Heiman training about that. None of the *Little Red Book of Selling's* 12.5 Principles of Sales Greatness discusses that. Nothing in *SPIN,* or *Selling to Big Companies,* or…. well, you get the picture.

That extra step of getting service inputs has ramifications for every part of the sales process, from prospecting to postclose follow up. And for those Services that can be "sold" with advertising, rather than a personal selling component, Sampson and Froehle's UST suggests there have to be differences in that advertising as well.

I thought that this "extra step" could account for many of the questions and paradoxes I'd encountered over my career. Here's one example:

When I was a business developer at Ipsos (a global market research firm), tasked with selling ad hoc custom market research services, I would call on prospective clients to introduce our work. As a research services company, every project was unique and undertaken in order to answer a specific business question. But the work did fall into categories: Pricing Research, New Concept Ideation, New Concept Testing, Feature Set Optimization,

Advertising Testing, and so on. We had clever names for these categories, which gave us something to advertise.[4]

Before I would go to appointments, the head of my division would sometimes ask the straightforward question, "What are you going to try to sell them today?"

I never knew how to answer, and there would always be moments of awkward silence. My answer would typically be something like, "Uh. Uh. I'm not sure yet." Sometimes he would press with, "Well, didn't you qualify them?[5] What is it they might want to buy?"

In fact, all I knew about companies like Merck or Hewlett Packard was A) that they spent tens of millions of dollars a year buying market research of every type and B) I wanted a slice of that budget.

At the time (this was pre-UST) I didn't have the language to describe what I was trying to do. I ended up giving cryptic, Zen-like answers that would have been more annoying if I didn't have consistently good results. I'd say things like, "The secret to selling them everything is not to sell them anything."[6]

---

[4] We'd give our "Products" names, even though we hadn't productized the offering. That way, we would have something to put on brochures when talking about our areas of expertise.

[5] Every sales training program stresses the importance of pre-qualifying early in the selling process. That means making sure that anybody you try to sell to has the right credentials to buy: Can afford it, is the decision-maker, has a need for your product or service, etc. The exception was my sales manager during the three years I sold life insurance. He said, "See the people. Some will buy. You have no way of knowing in advance which ones."

[6] Actually, it was because my results were so good that I could afford to entertain myself by offering cryptic Zen answers.

After I'd been doing it a few years and had a better understanding of what I was doing, I would explain that I was "selling them on the idea of sending us RFPs when they need work done." I didn't know it at the time, but what I was really saying was that I was trying to create a stream of service inputs on which we could base future sales.

It seemed that the goal of this first "sales presentation"[7] was not to sell something but to complete the un-named and un-discovered intermediate step of "get Service inputs."

What other mysteries associated with the world of Selling could be answered by considering the questions through the lens of UST? I was reminded of some of the paradoxes of sales that are not often talked about:

- 46%—almost half—of new salespeople fail in the first 18 months, according to Mark Murphy at Leadership IQ Corporation. Does that number seem high to you? According to Dave Kurlan at the Objective Management Group, that number is closer to 74%. And this is the case despite billions spent on recruitment, suitability testing, and professional sales training. Even successful salespeople flounder when they change industries. Could it be because they move from Products to Services (or vice versa) and don't know

---

[7] A.K.A Statement of Capabilities

they are experiencing a fundamental change that involves re-learning parts of their craft?

- When selling Products, a marketer can count the number of people who place an order, whether it's by clicking a "buy now" button or phoning a call center. But that doesn't work with Services. Marketing metrics for Service providers are much harder to conceptualize than for Product manufacturers. I've been in meetings where the VP of Marketing told the CEO that the goal of the marketing program was not to actually "make sales" but to "increase awareness." Therefore, if our call center got lots of requests for more information, then the ad campaign had been successful—even if no new sales could be tracked.

  Could you imagine a similar conversation with Vince from ShamWow?[8] How long do you think the ad campaign would have continued if, at the end of the first day, the CEO asked Vince how many chamois cloths he had sold that day, and the answer was, "Well, boss, it's like this: More than 20,000 people responded to my call to action to "Call now! Operators are standing by!" They were all really good conversations. None of those 20,000 callers actually placed an order, but we're pleased because we know we "increased awareness."

- Is there some other metric, related to UST definition of sales, that could let us better evaluate the effectiveness of a promotion program for Services? Maybe there needs to be an

---

[8] Google it.

intermediate metric like "quantity of service inputs received" rather than (or in addition to) "quantity of sales made."

- If a Service can't be sold without first receiving Service Input, then does a call to action have any meaning with a Service offering? Is there an equivalent to "Buy Now!" for Services?

I felt like Anthony Von Leeuwenhoek, who, armed with the newly invented microscope, could see blood cells and micro-organisms for the first time. My tool was UST, and I could use it to compare Services and Products properly for the first time.

What do I mean by "properly"? In April 1977, the world believed that there was a "spectrum of intangibility" that applied to Products and Services but that there was not necessarily a *difference* between Products and Services.

As a result, all the examination and thinking that was applied to Services marketing was handicapped by an incorrect definition. Without singling out any author, it could be said that everything that was written was *at least a little bit wrong*. Not because the researchers weren't the smartest in the field (because they certainly were) but because their work was based on incorrect predicates.

It was like a master carpenter who doesn't know that his tape measure isn't accurate.

There are countless books, articles, training videos, and seminars that look for ways to increase the sales of Services. Many compared Products and Services, and looked for similarities and differences. The problem was, without a clear definition, they couldn't properly tell the difference.

At one point, I was reading journal articles that tried to draw conclusions about how to market Services by comparing and contrasting the marketing practices of Products and Services. As I dug deeper, I realized that some of the papers contradicted each other when assigning the category "Product" or "Service" to an offering. One author labeled an offering a Service, and another labeled the same offering a Product.[9]

Reading the conclusions of the papers was like tasting cupcakes made by the world's finest pastry chefs who didn't know that some (but not all) of the sugar canisters contained salt, and some (but not all) of the salt canisters contained sugar. The world's brightest business minds were limited by bad definitions.

Keep in mind that you have it easy. You've already read Chapter Four-and-a-Half. You already know that there are four categories of things that can be sold. In addition to Products and Services, there are also Service-y Products and Product-y Services. Previous scholars hadn't seen these terms and had no way of knowing that some of the Products and Services they studied... weren't.

The reason I was reading all of these papers was that I had to choose a topic for my Master's thesis. I resolved to ensure that I faithfully used the "correct" definitions of Products and Services per Sampson and Froehle's Unified Services Theory. Regardless of the final scope of the project, I had two[10] over-arching goals:

---

[9] Remember Lynn Shostack's continuum? Each researcher had their own opinion about where on the Product-Service spectrum individual offerings belonged.
[10] Three, actually. I also wanted to earn my MBA.

- First, to see if UST was actually correct. That is, to see if the things UST predicted *should* occur in the marketplace actually *did* occur.
- Secondly, to build a list of best practices for advertising and selling Services. Since I was going to be the first person not to be handicapped by bad definitions, this thesis would be my secret weapon for making business decisions. I would know exactly how to write advertising for any Service I was selling. Perhaps I might even write a book.[11]

Direct response (DR) advertising is advertising that tries to get a buyer to take action toward a sale. They can be identified by a *Call to Action,* such as "Call now—operators are standing by!" or "Come in for a test drive today" or "If your portfolio currently holds more than $2 million and you'd like to see how your holdings would have fared if you had been managed by Gelden Haus Investments over the last five years, call to set up a meeting with one of our advisors."

If an ad isn't a DR ad, it's an "informational ad." Like all advertising, informational ads want to change behaviors, but they are not calling for direct action. For example, when you see a British Petroleum ad explaining how their oil rigs are actually good for the environment, BP wants you to feel good about their brand, but they aren't urging you to stop in to fill the tank on your car. There's no *call to action.*

---

[11] I guess it turned out that I *did* write a book.

I examined 734 direct-response advertisements in 83 English-language trade magazines from a wide variety of industries representing more than 40 verticals. My goal was to see if the calls to action for the Product ads were different from the calls to action of the Service ads. And if so, how?

The Products ranged in size from individual molecules to railroad locomotives. The value of the Services represented ranged from a few dollars to a few hundred thousand dollars. I wanted to make sure that my findings applied to *all* business-to-business[12] Services, in the same way that UST applied to *all* Services.

I categorized the calls to action according to 15 variables representing aspects of the sale and the marketing challenge. I recorded information like:

- What kinds of enticement were used to create urgency? Was it a free gift of some kind, a discount for quick action, or a threat of limited availability? For example, "Call before midnight tonight to receive 20% off." Did these enticements differ from Service ads to Product ads?

- Did the Calls to Action provide information? Or did the CTAs instead direct the buyer to get information from another source? An example of providing information (location) would be "Bring your car to Minute Muffler, 1315 Main Street," but an example of directing them elsewhere to get location information would be, "Visit our website to find the Minute Muffler near you."

---

[12] Since they were ads in trade journals, all were business-to-business.

I also recorded whether or not the ad even *had* a call to action. You might think that, by definition, a direct response ad *must* have a call to action, but the reality is that some are so poorly written that they are missing the all-important CTA. You can tell from the rest of the ad that the copywriter was leading up to a call to action but then chickened out at the last minute.

You probably saw the human-interaction equivalent to this in the hallway in high school. The conversation went like this:

Him:	So there's a big dance next Saturday night.
Her:	Yes, there is.
Him:	It looks like it would be fun to go.
Her:	Yes, I'd love to go, but nobody's asked me yet.
Him:	Yes. Uh. Well. Uh. Maybe I'll see you there.

The findings of my research are discussed in detail in Chapter Seven, but what I can tell you is that *the calls to action in Service ads were different in every measurable way from the calls to action in Product ads, and they differed in a way that could be predicted by UST.*

For example, UST suggests that a customer can't buy a Service without first providing service inputs. That means that it's nearly impossible for the customer to "Buy now!" or to "Click here to order."

Therefore, you could expect to see the following differences:

✦ Almost *all* Product ads would have a call to action, but almost *none* of the Service ads would have them.

- ▶ When a Service ad did have a CTA, its goal would be to get the customer to submit service inputs needed to advance the sales process. Since that is seldom practical in a B2B environment, you might expect the CTA to invite the buyer to a dialogue to discuss how to arrange the transfer of the SI to the provider. Product ads, on the other hand, can and did "cut to the chase" and urged the customer to make an immediate purchase.
- ✱ Since Products have set prices, their ads could brag about an especially good price and perhaps even offer a discount as incentive to make an immediate purchase. Services don't necessarily have pre-defined parameters, and that applies to pricing, so Service ads can't make the same kind of brags or offer the same kinds of discounts.

In fact, my research showed the following:

- ✦ 86% of Product ads—about 9 out of 10—had a clear call to action.[13]
- ✦ 68% of Service ads—about 7 out of 10—had *no call to action at all*.
- ▶ More than 20% of Product ads stated the exact price in their ads.
- ▶ Less than 1% of Service ads stated a price in their ads.

---

[13] 9 out of 10 had Calls to Action. What happened with the tenth ad? Sadly, the tenth ad saw the girl at the dance after all. She was dancing with a competitor who had a stronger call to action.

* The 5 most common words in the Product CTAs were:
  - Order
  - Offer
  - Specials
  - Today
  - An exact quotation of the price of the Product
* The 5 most common words in the Service CTAs were:
  - Learn
  - Find
  - Today
  - Contact[14]
  - The name of a specific technical expert who could intelligently discuss the service inputs

I made predictions about advertising based on Unified Services Theory, and those predictions turned out to be true. In the summer of 2010, I received my Master's degree in Business Administration from the University of Leicester. The thesis presented my research confirming that current business practices supported the utility of the UST paradigm.

Therefore, UST's definition of Products and Services was valid and worth serving as the basis for future thought.

Suddenly, we had a science.

---

[14] Or variations of making contact such as phone, call, email, etc.

I started rebooting everything I'd ever learned, examining the ramifications of UST on tactical issues of sales, advertising, and promotion.[15] I asked myself questions like:

If the process of selling Services requires SI, and the process of selling Products does not, then what does UST say about the nature of sales calls? Should the content of a Service sales presentation differ from a Product sales presentation? Or for that matter, what about prospecting, cold-calling, pitching, and closing? If so, how should they differ?

Consider the trope of the "pushy salesman". Does this mean that a Product salesperson would push when closing, but a Service salesperson would push when requesting service inputs?

Does that change how we track our sales opportunities? If we *need* a certain input (SI) to write a proposal for a Service, and we don't get that input, can we really call it an opportunity? After all, without the SI, we never really had a chance. Or maybe there needs to be a new term to discuss failure that results from not getting SI. Maybe sales organizations need to change the way they track progress through their sales funnel.

For example, The Miller Heiman Blue Sheet approach calls for using a "red flag" to denote anything that could interfere with making a sale. A list of red flags would include: being late to the bidding process; not knowing who the economic buyer is; your brand is not well known; and so on. But the most common red flags denote uncertainty or missing information. Perhaps there needs to be a name for a special red flag that denotes problems

---

[15] Admittedly navel-gazing, but navel-gazing by a person *with an MBA*.

with getting service inputs. This could be a lack of information about the SI at the quotation-writing stage, or an issue around providing the service, such as how you will get the broken jet engine to your jet engine repair facility.[16]

I've chosen Miller Heiman for this example because they are one of the best-known sales consulting groups, but I am sure that every sales consultant would benefit from incorporating UST into their checklists and processes.

It should be easy to see that all aspects of promotion, advertising, and selling should be reexamined in light of UST theory, even (and especially) the most accepted "best practices."

This book would have to be a hundred volumes long to examine every facet of the World of Sales and Marketing. Instead, we'll look at the some of the major buckets of business: Direct Selling, Human Resources, Advertising & Promotions, and Sales Management, and see what UST implies for these key areas.

Your experts, at your business, can integrate these major themes into your existing procedures. This is less of a "how to" book and more of a "what should" book. What should we be looking at in changing our hiring practices for the sales team? What should we track in order to evaluate our marketing processes? What should be included under the heading Desired Outcomes for our Service sales calls?

---

[16] The plane with the broken engine can't fly to your repair center because it has a broken engine.

Chapter Six

Not Two. Not Infinity. Exactly Four.

Unified Services Theory suggests that the sales process for Services includes an extra step that isn't required for Product sales, that is, getting the service inputs. Where does that extra step occur? Perhaps the extra step can be identified by comparing the two diagrams on the next page that illustrate "idealized" sales pathways for Products and Services.[1]

Consider any Product (not a Service-y Product, a regular Product); it could be a chocolate bar or a sports car.

The manufacturer makes the Product, and the marketing department promotes it. The word "promotion" in this case is meant to include every weapon in the armory of the professional marketer: TV ads, point-of-sale displays, a direct sales force, coupons, websites, viral videos, and so on.

---

[1] These are more complicated versions of the diagrams you saw in Chapter 5.

Product

- Value Add Phase
- Promotion
- Customer Gathers Choice Information (Products) ★
- Customer Compares Offers
- Final Selection and Payment

Service

- Promotion
- Customer Gathers Choice Information (Providers)
- Customer Provides Service Inputs
- Service Quotation
- Customer Compares Offers ★
- Final Selection and Payment
- Customer Provides Service Inputs
- Value Add Phase

LEGEND

⬡ Advertising/Promotion/ Selling Phase

◯ Purchasing Process Phases

▢ Service Inputs Phases

▢ Company Creates Value

☆ Offer Has Been Made by Seller and Available to Buyer

At that point, customers with wants and needs can gather information about competing offerings, compare them, and then make a purchase by informing the vendor of their final selection and making payment. You'll recognize that the only inputs provided by the customer to the seller are final selection and payment.

- *I'm standing in line in Walmart, and the array of chocolate bars reminds me I haven't had lunch yet. I notice a new kind of bar (Cadbury Marvelous Creations, with jelly beans and pop rocks) that I've seen advertised but have never tried. I mentally compare that to the usual kinds of bars I buy (Snickers, Fruit and Nut, Peanut Butter Cups, etc.) and provide the cashier with two inputs: The Marvelous Creations bar that I finally selected and payment.*
- *In this morning's paper, the review of the new Porsche made me wonder if I could afford a hot new car. I read online reviews and visit a few dealerships for test drives, speaking with several salespeople, who regale me with the benefits of their vehicle. I take the brochures home, read some more, and then finally go back to one dealership. The saleswoman points out that it was good that I came back quickly while there is still plenty of choice. I provide her with my final selection (the red one, 17" wheels, leather interior, etc.) and payment, which in this case is a check because I've already arranged financing from my bank.*

Despite the fact that one costs 100,000 times as much as the other, both the 50-cent chocolate bar and the $50,000 car

Product

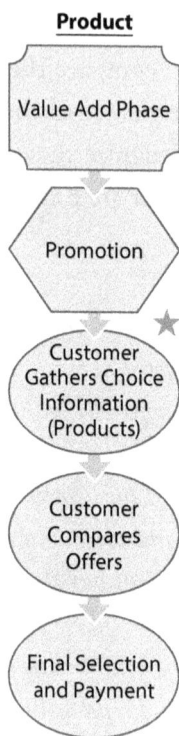

Value Add Phase

Promotion

Customer Gathers Choice Information (Products)

Customer Compares Offers

Final Selection and Payment

LEGEND

Advertising/Promotion/ Selling Phase

Purchasing Process Phases

Service Inputs Phases

Company Creates Value

Offer Has Been Made by Seller and Available to Buyer

follow exactly the same Product sale flowchart. This is exactly what UST predicts.

For both Products, the selling process looks like the diagram to the left.

On the other hand, consider any Service (not a Product-y Service, a regular Service), such as dry cleaning.

Unlike Product manufacturing, the first step isn't to "make" the Service. The Service can't be made until the buyer provides service inputs. Instead, the first step toward a sale is *promotion.*

For my neighborhood dry cleaner, promotion means an ad in the yellow pages, a three-story mural on the side of their building (which is located on a high-traffic road), in-mailbox fliers, and fridge magnets.

When my down comforter needed cleaning, I called them to find out how much it would cost. They had a million questions for me: How big was the quilt... twin, queen, or king? Was the down layer "heavy" or "light"? What was the cover made of? Was it light dirt or heavily stained? In the end, they suggested I bring it in, so I did. Once they examined it, they explained it would cost $60 to dry clean.

That struck me as a lot, so I phoned around to a couple of other dry cleaners, armed with the information (SI) from the first cleaner's analysis: It's a king-sized comforter, thick down, 100% cotton cover, dirty but unstained. I got quotes ranging from $45 to $65.

I didn't go to *every* dry cleaner in the city. I was selective and considered only the ones that were near my end of town, and who had not, in the past, ruined my favorite shirt.[2] I also rejected a store with a reputation for being very expensive. But in every case, it was each cleaner's *past promotional activity* that put them in my original consideration set. I didn't consider any cleaner that I'd never heard of and didn't know existed.

In the end, I paid the $60 to my "regular" cleaner, because I knew they did good work, and they were in my neighborhood.

To get my quilt dry cleaned, I had to submit service inputs twice. Once at the beginning, in order to get a price quote, and then again to actually receive the Service. The second submission was the quilt, in for cleaning.

For a Service like dry cleaning, the selling process looks like this:

The dry cleaner promotes, to attract customers. Some dry cleaners get to move on to the next step, and some fail in this first selling step.

---

[2] *Really? It doesn't look that bad. I think you could get away with it. Maybe if you keep your suit jacket buttoned all the time.*

Service

- Promotion
- Customer Gathers Choice Information (Providers)
- Customer Provides Service Inputs
- Service Quotation
- Customer Compares Offers ★
- Final Selection and Payment
- Customer Provides Service Inputs
- Value Add Phase

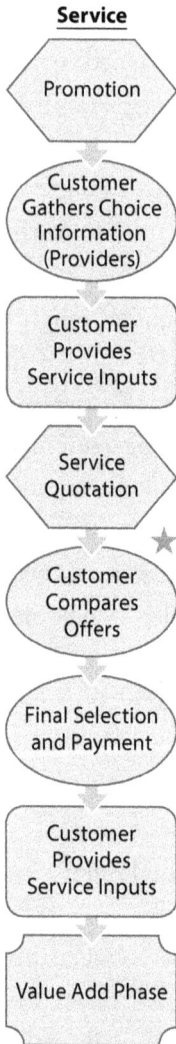

Once they have been selected as possible providers, the customer then provides service inputs (either the comforter itself or information about it). Once the dry cleaner has that Service Input, a quote can be prepared. The customer can then compare quotes, choose a dry cleaner, and bring the comforter in for cleaning. Only then can the dry cleaner do the work that adds value.

Taking laundry to the neighborhood dry cleaner is about as simple a Service a person can purchase. Unified Services Theory suggests that *all* Services—no matter how big or small—should follow the same selling paths.

Let's see if it holds for a complex business-to-business offering: Forensic Accountancy.[3]

LEGEND	
⬡	Advertising/Promotion/ Selling Phase
⬭	Purchasing Process Phases
▢	Service Inputs Phases
▢	Company Creates Value
☆	Offer Has Been Made by Seller and Available to Buyer

[3] "Forensic" means it can be applied to the investigation of a crime.

Not Two. Not Infinity. Exactly Four.

Practitioners of forensic accounting have to be experts in many areas beyond Accounting: they need to understand their client's industry, they have to be fluent in the business issues they are investigating, and they have to understand the laws of the jurisdictions in which their clients do business. For example, one practice may specialize in environmental damages for oil and gas clients operating in Libya, and another in auditing expense accounts in France.

The promotional processes of a multinational forensic accounting firm could include regional sales forces, a marketing department that maintains a complex website and writes press releases, and thought leaders who write white papers.

All of these promotional activities are designed to drive the prospective buyer to provide the first stage of service inputs: The firm wants a prospective buyer to provide information (SI) that allows the firm to provide a price quote. That information could include:

- Size and scope of the client firm: 200 employees or 200,000?
- Industry: Healthcare or Pipelines?
- Issue of Investigation: Accident Benefits, Construction Defects, or Cyber Risk?
- Region: Canada, Colombia, or Cambodia?

Typically, this information is provided to the firm in the form of a Request for Proposal, or RFP for short. The RFP would be

Service

Promotion

Customer
Gathers Choice
Information
(Providers)

Customer
Provides
Service Inputs

Service
Quotation

Customer
Compares
Offers

Final Selection
and Payment

Customer
Provides
Service Inputs

Value Add Phase

LEGEND

Advertising/Promotion/
Selling Phase

Purchasing Process Phases

Service Inputs Phases

Company Creates Value

Offer Has Been Made by
Seller and Available to Buyer

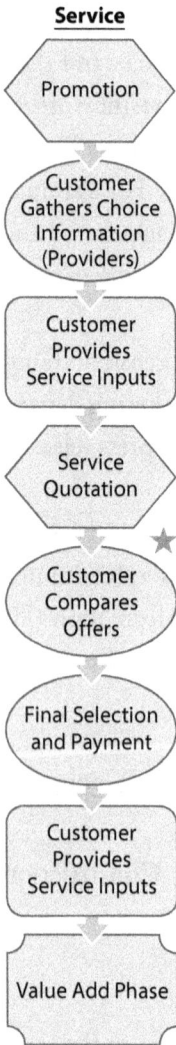

forwarded to a small number of competing service providers.[4] Each prospective vendor independently writes a proposal in the hopes of winning the business and submits it to the buyer.

Once the proposals arrive from the various forensic-accounting firms, they can be compared and one vendor chosen. The winner then receives further Service Input, in the form of actual financial records that can then be analyzed.

The two diagrams, showing the sales path for quilt cleaning and forensic accounting, are the same, just as predicted by UST.

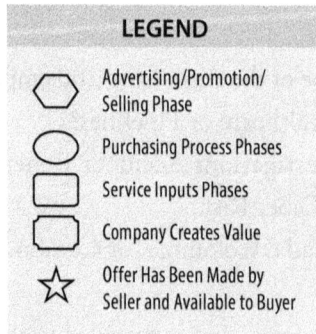

---

4. Less than 10, and often less than 5 vendors. Why so few? Wouldn't it make sense to get as many quotes as possible? Business-to-business proposals are *very* long. There is a limit to how much time a procurement team can spend reading similar—and often nearly identical proposals—without gouging their own eyes out in despair.

The differences between the two diagrams, Products and Services, are more than just the addition of the extra Service Input steps. Specifically:

Issue	Products	Services
Vendor adds value	At the very beginning	At the very end
How many promotional phases?	Only one promotional phase	Two promotional phases
What do promotions promote?	A well-defined Product offer of deliverables	Phase One: Promotes the service provider, not the service itself Phase Two: Promotes the quotation, which is, itself, a well-defined offer of deliverables
What is the goal of promotion?	Designed to drive sales	Phase One: Designed to drive initial service inputs Phase Two: Designed to drive sales
When does promotion occur?	Second step of process	Phase One: First step of process Phase Two: After receiving service inputs
Sales phases	Single sales phase can "close" the deal	First sales phase "sells" the idea of providing phase one service inputs. Second sales phase can "close" the deal.

Does this idea of "two sales phases" apply to any Service? Yes:

Service	Phase One Service Inputs	Phase Two Service Inputs
Airline Ticket	Information: name of traveler, Destination, and time frame	Person: the traveler
Courier Service	Information: destination, speed, size/weight of package	Property: the package
Construction	Information: blueprints, budget, timing, location	Property: land, construction materials, Information: local building codes, etc.
Education	Information: current level of ability, when and where available to study, transcripts	Person: the student
Investments	Information: level of risk aversion, investment preferences (or even hunches)	Property: money
Dentistry	Person: teeth for examination and diagnosis	Person: teeth for treatment

The idea that Services have two promotional phases is a new one. Let me be clear on the terms we're using to describe them:

Phase One Service Inputs (POSI): This is what the buyer gives to each prospective seller so that quotations for Service can be prepared. If you've received POSI, you're being considered. *The goal of a statement of capabilities is to get POSI.*

Phase Two Service Inputs (PTSI): This is what the buyer gives to one "winning" seller so the seller can provide the Service. This is the buyer's property, information, or person. *If you've received PTSI, you've won the sale. The goal of the proposal is to convince*

Service

Promotion

Customer
Gathers Choice
Information
(Providers)

Customer
Provides
Service Inputs

Service
Quotation

Customer
Compares
Offers

Final Selection
and Payment

Customer
Provides
Service Inputs

Value Add Phase

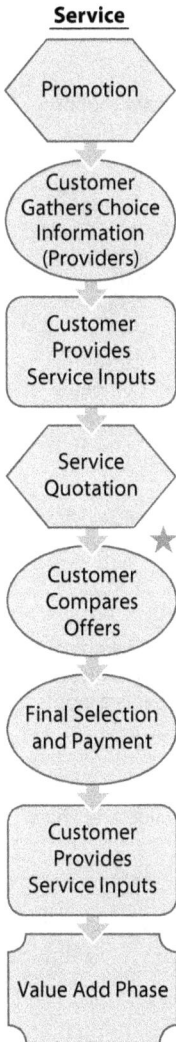

the buyer to select your proposal, make payment, and submit PTSI.

You are probably familiar with the business terms EBIT and EBITDA,[5] which are pronounced as EE-Bi-TEE and EE-Bi-DAH. The acronyms for Phase One Service Inputs and Phase Two Service Inputs are POSI and PTSI, respectively, and they are pronounced "Posey" and "Pitsey."[6] The "O" in Posey reminds you it's referring to phase *One,* and the "T" in Pitsey reminds you of phase *Two.*

Products and Services are two of the four categories discussed in chapter Four-and-a-half. What do the sales diagrams look like for Product-y Services and Service-y Products?

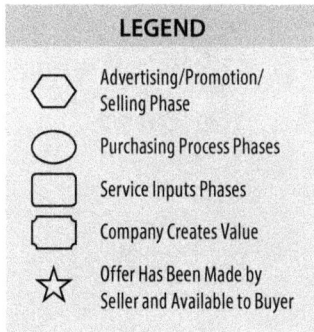

LEGEND

Advertising/Promotion/
Selling Phase

Purchasing Process Phases

Service Inputs Phases

Company Creates Value

Offer Has Been Made by
Seller and Available to Buyer

---

[5] Earnings Before Interest Depreciation and Taxes; Earnings Before Interest, Taxes, Depreciation, and Amortization
[6] Great names for pet gerbils.

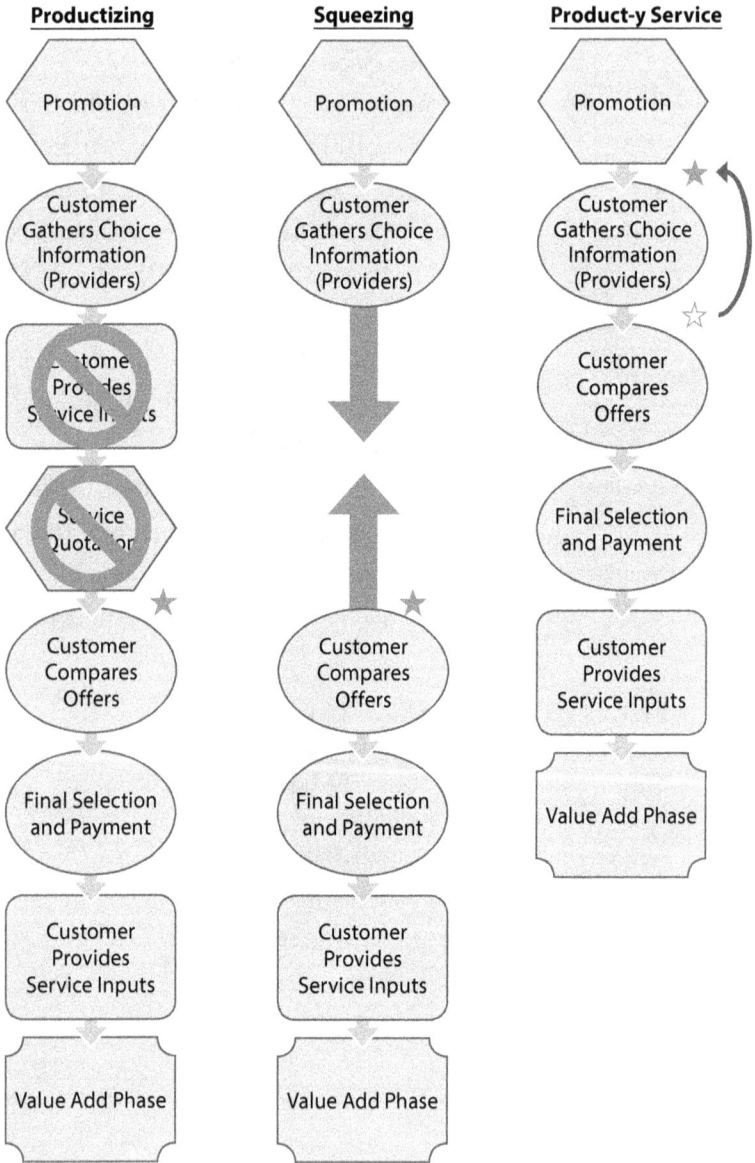

Productizing

Promotion

↓

Customer Gathers Choice Information (Providers)

↓

~~Customer Provides Service Inputs~~

↓

~~Service Quotation~~

↓ ★

Customer Compares Offers

↓

Final Selection and Payment

↓

Customer Provides Service Inputs

↓

Value Add Phase

Squeezing

Promotion

↓

Customer Gathers Choice Information (Providers)

⇓

⇑

↑ ★

Customer Compares Offers

↓

Final Selection and Payment

↓

Customer Provides Service Inputs

↓

Value Add Phase

Product-y Service

Promotion

↓

Customer Gathers Choice Information (Providers)   ★ ↰

↓ ☆

Customer Compares Offers

↓

Final Selection and Payment

↓

Customer Provides Service Inputs

↓

Value Add Phase

A Product-y Service, as discussed in Chapter Four-and-a-half, is a simplification of the regular Service pathway shown on page 99.

We already know that a Service can be productized by defining and constraining the service inputs. The vendor makes assumptions about the service inputs, and this eliminates two steps: the first service inputs (POSI), and the need to provide a personalized quote.[7]

On page 100, we squeeze out the eliminated steps, yielding the sales pathway for a Product-y Service.

Note that the star, representing when a concrete offer is made to the customer, has moved forward in the process, putting it just after the promotion stage. This is because the vendor has defined and constrained the service inputs and is therefore promoting an offer that includes all terms and prices.

On the next page, we'll compare the sales diagrams of a Product and a Product-y Service to prove that:

**A Product-y Service is a Service that is simplified[8]
so it can be sold the same way that a Product is sold.**

---

[7] Because the vendor is defining and constraining the service inputs, the vendor can assign a single price, and that price can be included in the promoted offering at the first step, for example, any dress shirt dry cleaned for $1.

[8] By the process of definition and constraint

This definition does not violate UST. Service inputs are still required to *provide* the Service, but it can be *sold like a Product,* without the "extra" first service inputs stage. In other words, by defining and constraining, the seller eliminates the need for POSI and can concentrate on getting PTSI.

This differentiation will be used in later chapters, to understand how sales presentations must be adapted to suit Products, Services, Product-y Services, or Service-y Products.

So far we've diagrammed the sales flow for three of the four offer types. What does the diagram look like for a Service-y Product?

Let's re-examine Rauland-Borg, makers of hospital communications equipment.

Rauland-Borg is a manufacturer, with a factory full of skilled engineers and modern assembly lines, located just outside Chicago. Their main business is clearly Product manufacturer.

Their sales channel consists of a trusted network of value-add companies that routinely call on hospitals to sell a variety of products such as IT and communications equipment, beds, surgical theatre lighting, and other durable, high-cost, capital equipment.

These distributors don't "make" anything. They don't produce products. However, the sales teams do more than just record the buyers' final selection of equipment and then take payment. They *provide expertise,*[9] based on their extensive experience.

The role of Rauland-Borg distributors, then, is not just to provide Product expertise but to help the buyer design their patient-care communications network. Their experience ensures that the

---

[9] Sounds like a Service to me…

Service

Promotion

Customer Gathers Choice Information (Providers)

Customer Provides Service Inputs

Service Quotation

Customer Compares Offers

Final Selection and Payment

Customer Provides Service Inputs

Value Add Phase

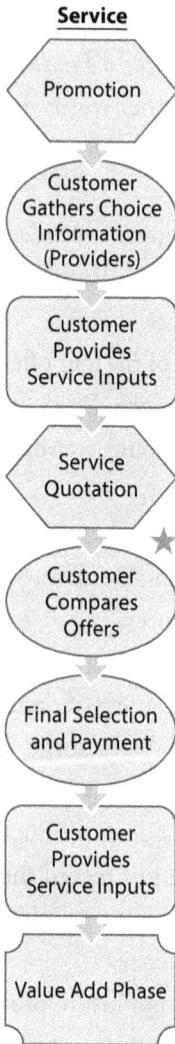

network integrates with the hospital, both from the standpoint of hardware (correct electrical junction boxes) and from the standpoint of human interaction (the number of beds being monitored by one nurse at a nursing station complies with local union rules).

For a Rauland-Borg distributor representative to write a quote, the prospective buyer must provide extensive service inputs. How many rooms/beds/nurse stations? Blueprints. Location. Availability of existing national infrastructure,[10] and so on.

From the standpoint of Rauland-Borg's distributors, the Service sales diagram (left) applies.

What is different in this case is that the Service isn't the main offering of the company. The main offering is a Product (communications equipment). The Service (communication network design consulting and installation) is added on to the Product. In fact, there's no direct charge for the design and expertise—it's built into the distributors' margins.[11]

---

[10] It's harder to build a hospital in countries with unreliable electrical service than with "developed" infrastructures.

[11] Rauland-Borg's competitors could not go to the distributors and ask for their help designing and installing a competing brand of equipment that they did not distribute.

We can therefore define a Service-y Product as a Product that adds a Service to its sales process. In other words:

A Service-y Product is a Product that requires an auxiliary Service to be sold and, so, is sold like a Service.

Even when the Service component of the offering is tiny compared to the Product component, that little bit of Service forces the need for service inputs, and so the sale of the Product is delayed until service inputs have been secured.

On page 106, the full-page diagram shows the complexity of Rauland-Borg's sales process.

There are two parallel sales tracks labeled Rauland-Borg (R-B). The first is the R-B Component track—which represents just the manufacturing department. The second sales track is the R-B Authorized Installer track—which corresponds to the sales and marketing track for new hospital installations. This track combines consulting and installation services with every purchase.

In the lower left corner is a list of some of the subprocesses involved in building a new hospital. Each represents a tangible Product (gas boilers, concrete floors, oxygen tanks) that is sold bundled with Services (expertise, installation, design, etc.).

Some of these subprocesses affect Rauland-Borg's quotation (e.g. blueprints and specifications for patient monitoring equipment).

Rauland-Borg resellers need that information to write their quotations. Therefore, from the R-B quotation perspective, information about those subprocesses are POSI.

POSI= *Phase One Service Input*   **PTSI**= *Phase Two Service Input*

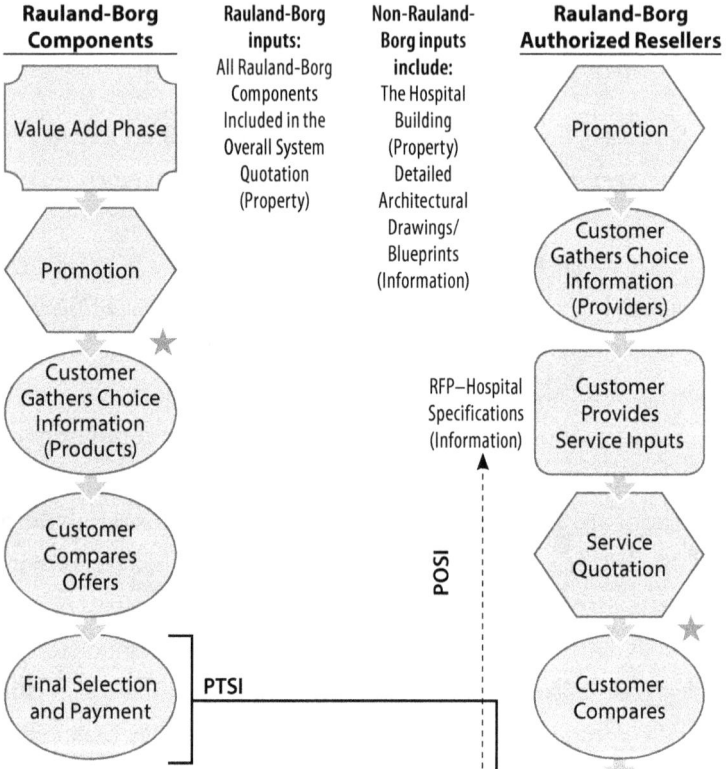

Rauland-Borg Components	**Rauland-Borg inputs:**	**Non-Rauland-Borg inputs include:**	**Rauland-Borg Authorized Resellers**

All Rauland-Borg Components Included in the Overall System Quotation (Property)

Non-Rauland-Borg inputs include: The Hospital Building (Property) Detailed Architectural Drawings/ Blueprints (Information)

Value Add Phase

Promotion

Customer Gathers Choice Information (Products)

Customer Compares Offers

Final Selection and Payment

PTSI

RFP—Hospital Specifications (Information)

POSI

Promotion

Customer Gathers Choice Information (Providers)

Customer Provides Service Inputs

Service Quotation

Customer Compares

Final Selection and Payment

Customer Provides Service Inputs

Value Add Phase

Building a Hospital Processes:
ARCHITECTURAL DESIGN Survey Site • Consultation with Stakeholders • Design • Prepare Blueprints ELECTRICAL Installation of Power Transformer Supplied by Manufacturers • Supply Grounding Protection • Install Distribution Electrical Panel FIRE SUPPRESSION AND SAFETY Install Fire Suppressor with CO2 • Install Safety Interlocks and Physical Barriers to Code • Train Staff • MEDICAL GASSES AND VACUUM Route and Install Sterile Lines or Oxygen, Nitrogen, Medical Air and Medical Vacuum COMMUNICATION AND CONTROL Cabling and Communication • Internet and Telephone Lines • Patient Monitoring and Telemetry FOUNDATION Design • Dig Foundation and Haul Away Debris • Pour Foundation and Piles Per Architect's Drawings • Pump Cement • Angle Bars • Paint Floor with Epoxy Paint • Concrete Compression Test Reports HEATERS AND BOILERS Supply and Install High Temperature Boiler • Thermal Oil Systems • Upgrade Gas Meter • Gas Lines and Regulator • Temperature Control Supply FRESH AIR AND EXHAUST Fresh Air Supply • Chimney and Vents for Burner • Exhaust Systems • Run Compressed Air Lines • Supply Air Duct Work • Insulation of Ducts WATER AND REFRIGERATION Supply and Install Chiller and Piping • Supply Water Line Process Piping

The dashed line shows where these other POSI feed into the R-B sales process.

Once the sales is made, the hospital organization (buyer) again provides service inputs. The solid line shows where PTSI feed into the sales process. For example, two PTSIs are the unfinished hospital building and the Rauland-Borg components which the installer has purchased on the hospital's behalf.

Rauland-Borg is a Product company. It promotes its Products like any other, for example, distributing brochures at trade shows and showing videos of nurses using the Products on their website. When Rauland-Borg promotes itself at international medical conferences, however, *its booth is actually in support of their local distributors.*

From Rauland-Borg's point of view, they offer a Product. They collect payment and provide the selected Products.

From the reseller's point of view, they offer a Service. They require service inputs from their clients to do a good job.

Here's a simpler example. Custom window manufacturers provide promotional material telling homeowners how their windows are better than their competitors' windows. But most don't offer to sell windows directly to homeowners, since most homeowners can't install windows themselves.[12] Instead, they tell buyers to "Insist on Our Brand windows" when they are talking to a contractor. The window manufacturer makes a Product, but the Product is tied to a Service, contracting.

---

[12] As a homeowner who has had new windows added to his home during an addition, and also watched as skilled tradespeople replaced old windows, I can tell you I'd be more comfortable taking out my own appendix than replacing a window.

Together, this hybrid is a Service-y Product. Like other Products, Roland-Borg and the window-maker have only a single promotional stage. For a "regular" Product, these promotional efforts would drive *orders* of the Product. In the case of a Service-y Product, these promotional efforts drive the submission of initial service inputs to the Sales and Installation track.[13]

This table summarizes the four kinds of fundamental offerings as defined by their POSI and PTSI inputs:

Category	Examples	Requires Phase One Service Inputs (POSI)	Requires Phase Two Service Inputs (PTSI)
Product	Shoes, TVs, Groceries		
Service	Forensic Accounting, House Painting, Plumbing	✓	✓
Product-y Service	Any shirt $1, FedEx Envelope, 3 rooms for $99		✓
Service-y Product	Rauland-Borg, Custom Windows	✓	

And the table can be visualized with the Service Inputs Product/Service Grid (SIPS). The vertical axis indicates if POSI is required or not, and the horizontal axis indicates if PTSI is required or not.

---

[13] Why don't window makers install what they manufacture? They would need to have installers in every city, and that would put them in competition with other contractors, who would never choose their brand of window. It makes more sense to focus on making the Product and let others focus on selling the Service. Even when you see ads for national companies that offer to install their products, the reality is that they quietly subcontract installation with a local provider.

Like the definition of a mammal, the SIPS Grid is a functional way to be certain which of the four categories an offering falls into. Ask two questions: Does it need POSI? Does it need PTSI?

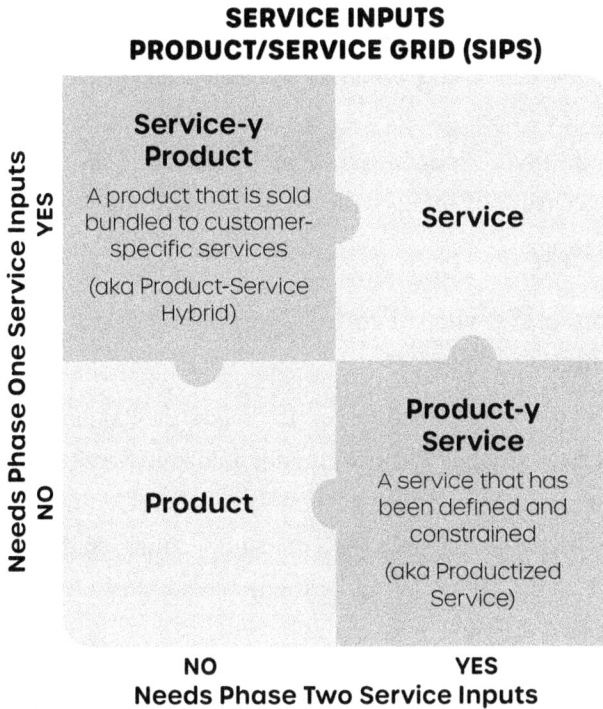

SERVICE INPUTS
PRODUCT/SERVICE GRID (SIPS)

	NO Needs Phase Two Service Inputs	**YES**
YES (Needs Phase One Service Inputs)	**Service-y Product** A product that is sold bundled to customer-specific services (aka Product-Service Hybrid)	**Service**
NO	**Product**	**Product-y Service** A service that has been defined and constrained (aka Productized Service)

Here, at last, are the less-cumbersome names for Product-y Service and Service-y Product:

Productized Service: A Service that has been defined and constrained. Productized Services do not require Posey during the sales process, but since they are Services, they require Pitsey once the sale is made, *so the provider can add value.*

Product/Service Hybrid: A Product that is coupled to a Service. Product/Service Hybrids are Products and can be manufactured without Posey or Pitsey, but because they are coupled to Services, Posey is required during the sales process.

And of course a **Product** is an offering that requires *neither* Posey *nor* Pitsey, and a **Service** is an offering that requires *both* Posey and Pitsey.

So it's not a Product/Service dichotomy, and it's not an infinite spectrum of intangibility—it's exactly four discrete kinds of offerings:

Products, Services, Product/Service Hybrids, and Productized Services

Products and Productized Services follow the Product sales path. Services and Product/Service Hybrids follow the Service sales path.

Your company's leadership must understand which of these your company offers. As we'll see in upcoming chapters, every aspect of the sales and marketing process has to be adapted to these two different sales paths in order to optimize your sales and profitability.

One other note regarding the four quadrants of the SIPS grid: Your business should consider moving your "usual" offering into other quadrants. These other quadrants can

- Serve as loss leaders, to make your Service more searchable on the web,
- Position you as a leader in a field

- Increase your market share and draw a fence around your client base
- Provide new sources of profits
- Identify opportunities for partnership
- Provide a "tangible" version of your Service to initiate discussions with potential clients

Here are two examples illustrating the relationship between the "original" offering and new offerings that could be developed by extension through the SIPS grid:

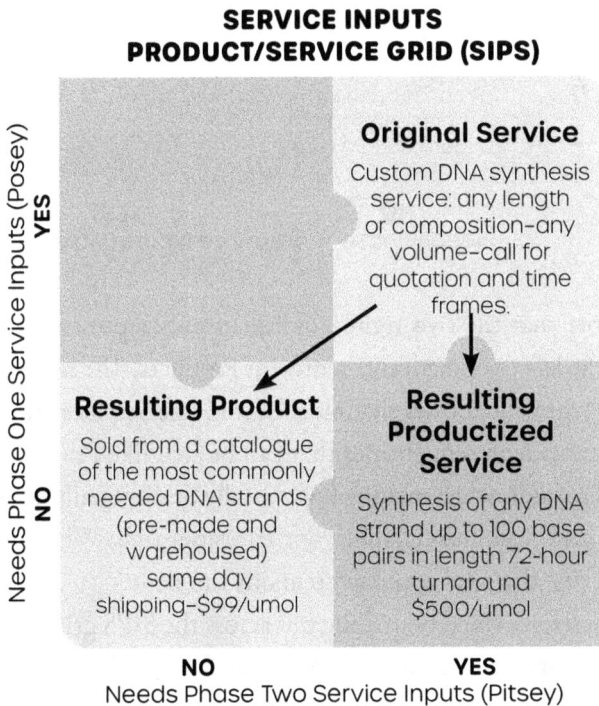

SERVICE INPUTS
PRODUCT/SERVICE GRID (SIPS)

Original Service

Custom DNA synthesis service: any length or composition–any volume–call for quotation and time frames.

Resulting Product

Sold from a catalogue of the most commonly needed DNA strands (pre-made and warehoused) same day shipping–$99/umol

Resulting Productized Service

Synthesis of any DNA strand up to 100 base pairs in length 72-hour turnaround $500/umol

Needs Phase One Service Inputs (Posey): YES / NO

NO / YES
Needs Phase Two Service Inputs (Pitsey)

SERVICE INPUTS
PRODUCT/SERVICE GRID (SIPS)

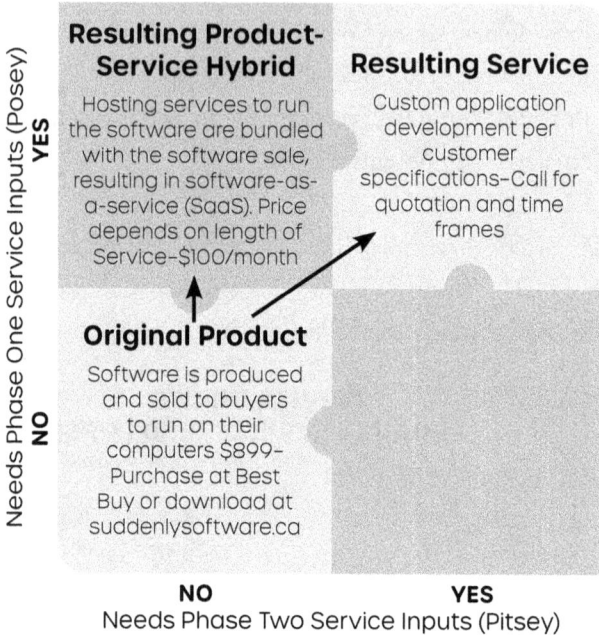

Needs Phase One Service Inputs (Posey)

YES

Resulting Product-Service Hybrid

Hosting services to run the software are bundled with the software sale, resulting in software-as-a-service (SaaS). Price depends on length of Service–$100/month

Resulting Service

Custom application development per customer specifications–Call for quotation and time frames

NO

Original Product

Software is produced and sold to buyers to run on their computers $899– Purchase at Best Buy or download at suddenlysoftware.ca

NO **YES**

Needs Phase Two Service Inputs (Pitsey)

Note that the two right-hand quadrants represent Services, and the left two quadrants represent Products. The upper quadrants represent entities that must be sold like Services. The lower quadrants represent entities that can be sold like Products.

As a result, when moving horizontally or diagonally across the SIPS grid, you must change your sales approach. When moving vertically, the sales approach remains the same.

Therefore, when branching out across the SIPS grid, you have to be aware that the sales process may change when you change quadrants, and your sales and marketing folks may have to be able to adapt their processes to the changed offering. As we'll discuss in Chapter Ten, that could mean hiring staff who are better suited to the new quadrant.

Chapter Seven

· ·

Two Sides
of the Same Coin?

When I teach Marketing to my first-year students, I differentiate between two definitions of "marketing"—what I term "Big M" and "Small M" marketing. "Big M" marketing pertains to the decisions made at the highest levels of the company. These are decisions about the nature of business the company will pursue, how it will make money, and how it will succeed against competitors. These are often defined by what are collectively called the 4P's of marketing, which, together, answer the questions

- What will we sell? (Product P[1])
- How much will we charge? (Price P)
- Where will customers buy our offering? (Place P)

---

[1] This is the P that defines what business you are in. Are you going to make shoes, make trucks to deliver the shoes, or be the delivery service that buys trucks to deliver shoes? Sometimes, the P is an S.

- How will our customers learn about our offering? (Promotion P)

Promotion, the last P in the list, is the responsibility of the Marketing Department. In most organizations, it's a misleading name because the primary function of the Marketing department is advertising or other communications that present the company's messages.[2] This is what I term "Small M" marketing: advertising and corporate communications. That is, brochures and billboards, television ads and Twitter feeds.

Technically, selling is a subset of the overall promotional function (salespeople promote through their personal activities), but the sales function and Small M marketing are usually separated because they require different expertise. The two are often spoken in the same breath (sales and marketing) as though they are the same thing, but I view them as *opposite* sides of the same coin. For example, salespeople don't usually have to know to how read an advertising rate card, and copywriters are not expected to cold call. My belief is that, in a "properly constructed" organizational chart, the Sales Team and the Marketing Team would roll up separately into a broader Promotions department.

For the balance of the chapter, when referring to "marketing,"[3] we'll be talking about "Small M" marketing, meaning advertising and promotions. These activities might support sales efforts,

---

[2] Press releases, policy comments, announcements about the "improvements" to the pension plan, etc.

[3] Regardless of whether it's capitalized or not

but it won't include the Sales team. We'll view sales activities as separate from marketing activities.

Why is this differentiation important?

Because each of the two departments, Sales and Marketing, is relevant at a different point in the Services selling process.

You may be sick of these two diagrams already, but there are some very important conclusions that can be drawn from them. For your convenience, they are found on the next page.

The differences between the two diagrams, Products and Services, are more than just the addition of the extra Service Input steps. Specifically:

Products (and by extension, Productized Services) have a single promotion phase. In this promotion phase, the Product and its tangible attributes—including price—are offered to buyers.

Services (and by extension, Product/Service Hybrids) have two very different promotional phases. The goal of the first promo phase is to drive buyers to provide the service inputs needed to create a quotation for delivering the Service. This kind of work, reaching out as broadly as possible to entice the entire population of potential buyers, is best suited for the Marketing Department. The Marketing Department is responsible for outreach through advertising, scheduling trade-show booths, and the like.[4]

---

[4] The Marketing Department may have a larger scope to its mission. Corporate communication is more than advertising to buyers. Corporate communication includes managing the perception of the company and its offerings in the minds of all stakeholders. These stakeholders include employees, investors, regulating agencies, and even, in the case of "reputation," the public at large. That said, for the purposes of this chapter, when we speak of the Marketing Department, we are concerned with advertising to customers.

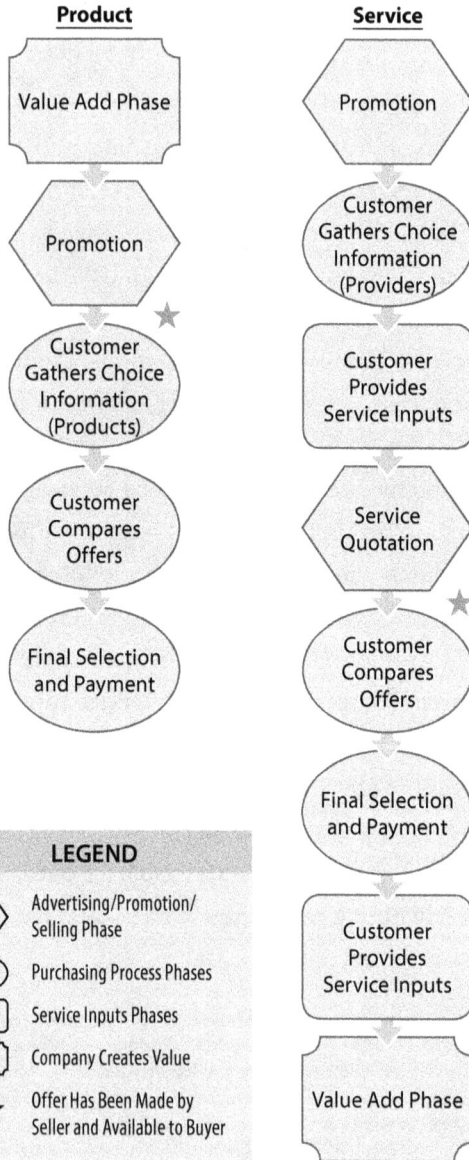

Product

- Value Add Phase
- Promotion
- Customer Gathers Choice Information (Products) ★
- Customer Compares Offers
- Final Selection and Payment

Service

- Promotion
- Customer Gathers Choice Information (Providers)
- Customer Provides Service Inputs
- Service Quotation
- Customer Compares Offers ★
- Final Selection and Payment
- Customer Provides Service Inputs
- Value Add Phase

LEGEND

Symbol	Description
⬡	Advertising/Promotion/Selling Phase
◯	Purchasing Process Phases
▢	Service Inputs Phases
▢	Company Creates Value
☆	Offer Has Been Made by Seller and Available to Buyer

In the second phase of promotion, the goal is to drive individual buyers to purchase the Service. This is best done on a one-to-one basis, working closely with the customer to fine-tune the offering, and in general trying to "close the sale." This kind of work is best suited to the "Sales Team."

You'll notice there are quotation marks around the words "Sales Team" at the end of the last paragraph. In the case of professional services, sometimes the only sales team is the professional who actually provides the service. In the case of B2B consultancies, this is known as the "service what you sell" or "eat what you kill" model. If a Service provider can't "land the clients," they will have no revenues with which to support the practice.

Therefore, the goal of the Marketing Department is simple: to garner the Phase One Service Inputs needed to advance the sales process. All measurements of the Marketing Department's effectiveness can be related back to that goal. Did we increase or decrease POSI compared to last year? How did promotional strategy "A" compare to promotional strategy "B" in garnering POSI? Did advertising medium X, Y, or Z result in the highest POSI?

How should a company define and track Phase One Service Inputs? That will vary from company to company and offering to offering. As guidelines, the following rules apply:

- The POSI must be of sufficient quality that it can lead to a sale. That is, the customer must be "qualified" to buy.
- The POSI should provide *everything* needed to write the sales quotation.

- The POSI process should create an expectation in the customer that they are instigating a sales process.
- POSI should include a timeframe for a response.

If the POSI does not meet these criteria, it should still be recorded, but only as a "failed" POSI event.

The POSI measurement can be based on whatever is the correct POSI that meets the criteria:

- Number of RFPs
- Number of dirty shirts
- Number of "free initial consultations"

The concept of incorporating POSI into ROI calculations is new. Historically, promotional success has been measured as a function of demand generation, that is, as a measurement of how well the promotion drove awareness of, and interest in, the vendor's offerings.

For example, let's say that a given promotion with a budget of $100,000 generated 38 inquiries about an offering that sells for $50,000. It could be said (perhaps by the head of the Marketing Department) that their activity had resulted in potential sales of $1.9M, a return of 19:1.

A more conservative manager might point out that seven of the inquiries were from buyers too small to actually buy anything, three were tire-kickers who have wasted our time before, and one was from a competitor scoping us out. That means 27 useful POSI events resulting from the campaign and 11 other inquiries that did not result in useful POSI events. The 27 useful POSI events represented $1.3M of prospective revenues, for an ROI of 13:1, revenues to expenditures.

Which seems like a fairer way to measure return on the promotion? 19:1 or 13:1? 1900 percent return, or "only" 1300 percent return?

I would argue *neither*. Let's follow the scenario of the 38 inquiries through to the end. We put the 27 useful POSI events into our proposal-writing process, and we were able to get all 27 proposals out by the clients' decision deadlines. We had a total of 10 wins (37% win rate) resulting in $500,000 in sales.

But the $500,000 represents *gross* revenues. I'm going to define the margin on these sales as 50%, so the $500,000 in revenue represents $250,000 in profits.

Should we say that the promotional activity resulted in $500,000 of return, or $250,000? I would argue that *profit* is the correct metric against which to balance the *risk of expenditure*.

From this, a series of metrics for measuring return on investment for the Marketing Department can be defined:

$$\text{Marketing ROI} = \frac{\textit{Returns resulting from POSI events} - \textit{Costs of generating POSI events}}{\textit{Costs of generating POSI events}}$$

A company has to define "returns" and "costs" in the above equation according to what makes sense to them, but here is how I would have calculated ROI on this example:

We've said the ad campaign had a $100,000 budget, so managers might want to say the cost was $100,000. But there are other considerations. What is the overall overhead cost of the marketing department? If annual overhead is $600,000, and half the staff's time is spent on business-development output,[5] and the campaign lasted for two months out of the year, then the overhead allocation to the campaign would be ($600,000) x (0.5) x (2/12) = $50,000, plus the expenditures related to the ad campaign ($100,000), so the overall cost of the campaign is actually $150,000.

And the returns? We've said our imaginary campaign generated 38 inquiries composed of 27 useful POSI events and 11 other inquiries that did not result in useful POSI events. The 27 useful POSI events resulted in 10 wins totaling $500,000 representing $250,000 of profit.

Marketing ROI= $\frac{\$250,000-\$150,000}{\$150,000}$ = 67% return on investment. That's a hugely different number than the 1900 percent return show by conventional metrics.

Is that 67% return "fair" to the Promotion Team? After all, the argument could be made that their job is to generate *inquiries* and that it's not their fault if the sales team isn't able to close the business. I think that is a spurious argument. Unless there is overwhelming evidence that the sales team is incompetent—and that situation is usually pretty obvious—then it raises the question, "What's going wrong?"

That discussion has to look at both the Sales and Marketing efficiencies, separately and together, and ensure that all the gears in the bigger machine are meshing correctly. Is the marketing activity soliciting POSI from the correct buyers? Are the POSI

---

[5] ...and the other half on internal communications, stockholder relations, and other non-revenue-generating activities.

events being properly handled internally, with good interdepartmental communication? I know one large company where the employees have a term, "eaten by the machine," meaning that an otherwise "winnable" opportunity was lost because of infighting over which division or sales team would respond to the POSI.

I think the correct way to judge Services marketing effectiveness is to first count the number of *useful* POSI events that result from a campaign. That tells us whether the campaign succeeded or failed to engage with prospective buyers. Secondly we have to consider the actual revenues generated by the campaign. That tells us if the Marketing and Sales teams are meshing.

Your managers should sit down together to create metrics that are relevant to your company's processes. These metrics should identify and evaluate each step of your Service-offering pipeline. Did the ad drive dialogue? Did the dialogue garner POSI? Did the POSI suggest you could write a winnable proposal? Were your internal systems set up to quickly and effectively respond with a proposal? Did you win the proposal? At each step, there should be a measure of effectiveness in much the same way as the various parts of a sales funnel are evaluated.

These metrics can be applied to each individual aspect of your marketing process: trade shows, cold calling by a senior partner, sending junior staff to Chamber of Commerce lunches, radio ads, etc.

Remember that Sales and Marketing are two sides of the same coin, rolling up into a broader Business Development/Promotions function. It is fair to demand the same ROI measurements from the Marketing Department as are expected from the Sales team.[6] Every salesperson has his or her closing rate recorded, so I don't think it is unfair to hold the Marketing staff to similar metrics. Salespeople have sayings like, "The commission rate on losses is zero." I think the marketing people should be expected to have the same culture. Everybody should be on the same page.

The job of the advertising department for a Service company is similar to the job of a Product company in that advertising is a one-way communication between the marketing team and the prospective buyer. Where the roles differ is in the purpose of the advertising: Product ads want the buyer to buy; Service ads want the buyer to provide service inputs.

What about the role of salespeople? Does it also differ from Products to Services? Let's look at *their* processes more closely.

The star in the sales-process diagrams indicate the point at which an offer to sell something is being made to the buyer. At first glance, it looks like the Service offer comes at a completely different point in the process from the Product offer. But does it really?

Consider what a quote to provide a Service looks like:

It details what service will be provided, quantities, the time frame for delivery, the scope of the process, the cost, and so on. The Service quote looks very much like a Product description.

---

[6] For the department as a whole, for individual campaigns, and for individual business-development activities. Which is a more efficient driver of sales—trade-show booths or golf dates with clients? Track POSI, and you'll know what works best.

Product Description	Service Quotation
Egg carton model Clck-12 holds 2½ dozen eggs (30). Interlocking tabs on the top and bottom of the tray allow up to 10 trays to be stacked without putting pressure on the eggs in the bottom tray. Corrugations ensure fewer than 1% of eggs are broken in transport. Cost per tray is $0.40 each for small quantities, $0.30 for orders of more than 100, and may be picked up at 228 Main Street during the hours of 9am–5pm	We will dry clean your pleated skirt, repair the little tear near the zipper, individually iron all 30 pleats, and return it to you on a padded skirt hanger wrapped in plastic. You can pick it up on Wednesday at our storefront at 230 Main Street. The cost of the repair, cleaning, and pressing will be $12.50

In fact, when a service provider writes a quote to provide a service based on the client's ad hoc service inputs, the first step is to treat the service inputs as a constant for that engagement. What had been a variable is now a constant.

In other words, when writing a Service quotation, the provider allows the *customer* to define and constrain the service inputs.

Do those terms seem familiar? They should. "Define and constrain" is the one-step process for productizing a Service.

A Service quotation is, de facto, a Product offering. The buyer compares it to other quotes on the basis of its features, benefits, and price, just as with any other "Product."

Here are the purchase flowcharts again, this time focusing in on the "decision to buy phase."

The two processes are almost identical, and can be summarized this way:

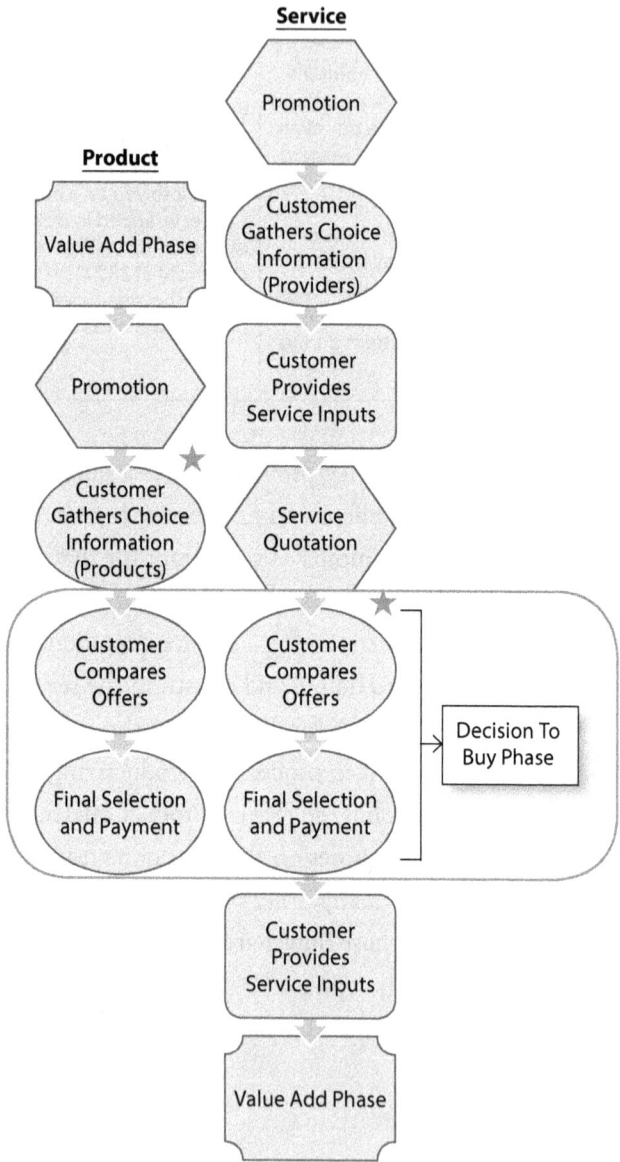

- Offers have been made by the sellers, and these offers have been collected by the buyer.
- The buyer compares each offer.
- The buyer selects the best offer.

The star represents a concrete offer to sell something specific and does not require further service inputs to close the sale at this stage. The Service can be purchased, as though it was a Product, *even though* it's a Service.

What that means is that everything a Product salesperson might do to "close" a Product sale applies to a Service sale, once the quote has been delivered. So while the activities of Service and Product salespeople differ at many stages of the sales process, *once the proposal is written, the job is very much the same.*

My experience has been that very few Service providers, especially B2B professionals, know that they can and should be using "conventional" (meaning Product) closing techniques once the proposal is delivered.

To circle back to the first page of this chapter, the Sales Team and the Marketing Team have different jobs, and their specialized skills will be utilized at different points in the sales process. The Marketing team is responsible for attracting POSI so the sales team can write proposals. Once the proposal is written, it constitutes a tangible offering, with features and benefits, that the Sales team can then sell, using similar techniques that would be used in selling any other Product.

Chapter Eight is directed to the Marketing Department and provides strategies and approaches for advertising Services, with the goal of garnering POSI. This content is based on my research examining hundreds of Service ads.

Chapter Nine is directed to the salesperson and provides strategies and approaches for writing the Service offering and closing the Service sale. This content is based on my experiences selling Services over the last 25 years.

Chapter Ten is directed to the HR people responsible for hiring and training salespeople.

Chapter Eight

Ten Rules for Service Advertisers That Won't Make Any Sense if You Start Reading the Book Here

Based on my research that examined Calls to Action in 700+ business-to-business ads across more than 40 verticals, I've assembled 10 rules for Service advertisers. As discussed in Chapter Four-and-a-half, these apply to Services and Service/Product Hybrids, that is, for Products that need to be marketed like a Service.

Rule One: All Service ads should have a Call to Action

If your purpose in creating a promotion process is to drive business, then that process should contain a call to action. Whether the promotion involves Twitter, a paper brochure available in a trade-show booth, a text message, or a billboard, you need to have a CTA. The CTA is the difference between driving business and wishful thinking.

Keep in mind that the goal of a good call to action is either to direct the buyer to make a purchase or to move the buyer down the buying path and closer to making a purchase.

My research showed that few Service ads have a call to action, even though the ad was definitely trying to drive sales. In the place of a solicitation of Service Input, many ads tried to get a dialogue going, using a phrase similar to "Give us a call" without actually explaining that the purpose of the call was to provide service inputs.

The American comedian Jerry Seinfeld has a stand-up comedy routine in which he discusses the phenomenon of men in cars sitting at red lights and honking their horns at attractive women as they walk by. He points out that never in the history of dating has a woman ever been attracted by a man honking at her. But the men, Jerry explains, know they need to be doing something, anything, to begin the dialogue that will lead to a date, and so they sit fruitlessly honking at women.

So, too, the marketing teams at Service companies urge buyers to "Call us!"[1] They know they are supposed to begin a dialogue of some kind, but they're collectively not sure what the call to action should look like.

---

[1] Call, write, email, etc. Get the dialogue going.

Make sure that your ad contains a call to action that will ultimately result in POSI.

Rule Two: The direction of the information flow in the CTA should be *to* you, not *from* you.

The CTA should drive POSI. One of the basic questions I had in my research was "If the Service ad has a call to action, does it ask the customer to provide Phase One Service Input?" What I found was that only about 10% of Service ads specifically asked to continue the conversation in a way that provided POSI. The other 90% either did not have a CTA at all or had a CTA that was so weak as to be pointless.

For example, "Visit our website for more information" is a bad CTA. At that moment, you have the buyer's attention and *could* be getting the POSI you need to begin the selling process. Providing more general information from your website is the *opposite* of what you need to be doing at this point.

The stronger approach is to give the buyer a reason to initiate a dialogue and to make sure it's a dialogue that provides the service inputs needed to drive the sales process forward.

My research examined the idea of "location information" provided in the ads. Product ads direct buyers to the *location* where they can make an immediate purchase, whether that is a storefront, website, or catalogue phone center.

Let's generalize the idea of "location" to include any place in time or space where a dialogue to garner POSI can take place. This could include a face-to-face visit, online chat, phone call, email, etc. But the important thing is that the CTA has to specifically create the expectation that the customer will have to provide POSI. Otherwise the encounter is wasted.

Here are some examples of CTAs that ask for POSI and give the coordinates where the transaction can take place:

- Our work begins with your business challenges. Call XYZ to share your story.
- Use this online form to book a time to talk to one of our experts. We'll listen carefully to your issues and explain how XYZ can help resolve them.
- It may be less expensive than you think. Bring your ABC in to 234 Main Street, and let us give you a free quotation.
- Just give us your address, and we'll have one of our technicians examine your ABC. We'll provide you with a detailed, no-obligation estimate specific to your ABC environment. You can reach us at (204) 891-1891 or at "HereIsMyAddress.com"

That last example actually directs buyers to a website, something I told you not to do just a few paragraphs ago. Can a website gather POSI? Yes!

At one time, I owned www.IAmApplying.com, which consisted of an online form through which loan applicants could provide POSI to a loan broker. *There was nothing else on the site.* It existed solely to collect POSI. All of the company's other marketing materials (brochures, website, etc.) directed borrowers to the POSI website, or, if they had a specific question, to a human being. Sending customers to other kinds of websites may provide *them* with general information, but does not provide you with the POSI needed to advance the buying process.

Here is an example of a CTA that implies the buyer will have to provide POSI without explicitly mentioning it:

- XYZ Accounting built our reputation by helping our clients make good decisions in complex situations. Call today, and let one of our CMAs help you find the most profitable answers.

The unspoken phrase "… to your business questions" didn't need to be added to "most profitable answers."

Rule Three: When possible, give an exact price.

More than 20% of all Product ads gave a set price, often expressed as part of a special deal. As we already know, it's impossible for a Service ad to provide an exact price until the specifications of the Service are defined through service inputs. It's no surprise then that less than 2% of all Service and Service/Product Hybrids ads offered exact prices.

But is that how things have to be? There would be a huge psychological advantage to be willing to discuss price in your ads when your competitors are not. If a prospective customer looks at a few websites and sees prices (especially reasonable prices) on only one website (yours), it makes your business stand out as approachable. It lets buyers know if you are in their "price range" or not and reduces their risk that they will begin a discussion about something they cannot afford.

Here are two ways my research showed Service offerings can be adapted to provide a "deal" in their advertising:

1. A Service can be productized through the "define and constrain" approach. The resulting Product can be given an appealing price and provide a concrete starting point for discussions about Services.

   You've probably seen this in the legal field with lawyers offering to write a will for newlyweds for a set fee. The lawyer knows the young couple will probably need legal services on an ongoing basis, when buying a home, starting a business, resolving a parent's estate, and so on. In this case, the loss leader gets the new clients through the door.

   Any subset of the overall basket of services can be the basis for define and constrain. A lawyer could have just as easily provided a set price for an incorporation, a house purchase, etc.

   By the way, Service providers can be just as sneaky as Product providers when it comes to pricing. I know of one company that productized a highly creative Service offering. It seemed like a great price, and it did drive inquiries from new customers. However, as their head of sales explained to me, "Nobody ever bought it. We'd designed it to look great on paper, but it never met anybody's *exact* need. Once the dialogue started, it always turned out that they needed something else. But we started the relationship wearing a low-cost halo."

2. Another sneaky trick is to provide a set price for the *introductory* stage. Brainstorming. Landscape design. Diagnosis. Preliminary.... you name it. When the Check Engine light goes on, a car owner needs a special code reader to understand what is happening with the engine. Mechanics offer to read the code for a low price, and many advertise that they will do it for free. That introductory step provides them with all the POSI (a vehicle with a problem) to advance the sale of their services.

So to recap Rule Three, contrive to offer a set price.

Rule Four: Make a special offer.

To make calls to action more effective, Product marketers often offer a *sales promotion* to make the basic offering more compelling and time sensitive. There are several categories of sales promotions, but the major "buckets" would include:

- Price reduction, aka, a discount: coupons, percent off, dollar amount off, rebates, and bundling
- Bonus: a gift that is the same as the main merchandise being purchased. A small free bottle of the distillery's premium gin attached to the larger bottle of their gin.
- Free Gift: a gift that is different from the main good being purchased. Free hot dogs to everybody visiting the car dealership on July 4th Weekend, or a box of margarita mix when purchasing a bottle of tequila.

- Free Sample: a sample of the main product provided in advance of the main product being purchased. Samples engage the buyer and reduce the "fear" of an unfamiliar offering.

Product companies use these sales promotions as leverage to get the buyer to make a purchase "now."

I regularly receive flyers from Popeye's Supplements, a national retailer that caters to bodybuilders and athletes. I remember a great ad for a product they carried, *Gaspari MyoFusion Probiotic.*[2] It was memorable because it offered so many incentives:

- New Year's Eve promotion available only from January 2nd to February 24th. **(Time Urgency)**
- Regular cost of one bottle is $80. During the promotion, you can buy one for $70 **($10 off Price Reduction),** or buy two for $120 **(Bundling for a price discount of $20 off each bottle)**
- Free AminoLast with purchase of MyoFusion—a $10 value **(Free Gift)**

The final call to action, intended to drive buyers into their stores, closes with:

---

[2] A dietary supplement composed of powdered protein enhanced with healthy bacteria

- Visit any Popeye's Supplements location and see for yourself how good it tastes **(Free Sample)**

The ad works because it creates urgency with a limited-time price-discount offer, sweetens the deal with a free gift, and pre-empts purchases from online competitors by offering a free sample.

All of the above insight can be found in any first-year marketing textbook. The rules for a call to action are pretty straightforward when your Product is a Product.

Let's discuss what these look like when your Product's not a Product.

Special Offers—Free Gifts

Free gifts differ from free samples in that they are different from the main service being offered. If a dentist offers a free checkup for new patients, that's a sample. If the dentist offers a free iPad with every root canal, that's a free gift.

Keep in mind that the goal of the free gift is to advance the sales process by either directly soliciting SI or by acting as a stepping-stone to SI. The free gift should, at the very least:

- Get the buyer's contact information
- Provide information about the buyer's situation and what the solution set might include
- Ensure there is a reason to continue the conversation past "Thanks for the free gift, and goodbye"
- Ensure the buyer understands there will be further conversation

Here is what the research showed were the most common kinds of free gifts offered by Service companies:

- **An actual, free, tangible gift.** These are the weakest because they acquire only the most general service inputs. Careful selection of your free gift will serve to qualify the prospects who respond. Here are some I saw while doing my research:
    - Statistical software (The service provider was targeting scientists who use statistical software.)
    - Book related to the field of the service being offered (Free copy of Elements of Design offered by a web design company)
    - Subscription to daily legal news summary (From a Labor Law consultancy)

Each of these gifts was selected to attract a very specific kind of buyer.

Be careful that the tangible gift is relevant, ethical, and not *so* valuable that it will entice non-prospects out of the woodwork. I remember getting emails from salespeople that were offering me $100 to listen to their sales pitch. They were "so confident" that I would be interested in purchasing that they were willing to risk that much money. That fails on so many levels. To me, it indicated marketers who couldn't craft a succinct benefit statement, and who didn't understand that most employers forbid their buyers from taking cash gifts from salespeople.[3]

---

[3] Most employers and many penal codes.

There was one free gift that I thought deserved an award of some kind—A Starter Kit.

When a dentist can't save a tooth, the tooth is removed, and a replacement tooth is crafted to take its place. This replacement can be a denture, a dental implant, or a crown. Making the crown is a skilled craft unto itself. The dentist takes all the measurements and makes a mold of where the replacement tooth must go. That service input is then couriered to the dental lab, where the replacement is made. The new tooth—and the patient—then return to the dentist's chair so the new tooth can be fine-tuned for comfort and fit.

All of the advertisements for dental labs in my study offered free shipping back and forth to the dentist's office. One of the labs, however, offered to provide a small cabinet specifically designed to hold courier envelopes. The cabinet came filled with pre-paid envelopes *pre-addressed to the dental lab*. On the front door of the cabinet (which was of very high quality and very attractive) was a small plaque that read "Running out of courier packs? Call…" followed by the number of the dental lab.

What an elegant solution! It solved the office manager's problem of where to keep the courier envelopes and made submitting molds to the dental labs as easy as possible. This completely preempts the competitors. I pictured the dental-lab rep coming in to refill the cabinet every month or two and bringing in donuts and coffee for the office staff as well.

The call to action was simple: Call today to receive a free starter kit for ABC Labs, and we'll give you a free cabinet to keep your dental lab courier supplies in. This is a $300 value absolutely free. If you decide you don't like our services, you can keep the cabinet to keep our competitors' supplies in.

- **White papers and other thought-leadership publications related to the service being offered.** These solicit SI *indirectly,* based on the assumption that only qualified prospects would be interested in the white paper's topic. For example, only an institutional investor would be interested in a white paper on institutional investments. Therefore, a person who requests that paper automatically qualifies themselves.

  Here are some very specific white-paper titles that my research uncovered. By suggesting a solution to a problem, they open the door to communication:

  - Risk-Free Financing for Small Businesses
  - Turbulent Markets—Risks and Opportunities for the Institutional Investor
  - Composites and Remanufacturing—Meeting the Challenges of New Engine Designs
  - Reducing Membership Churn in Your Online Community Panel

  Remember the goal of any free gift is to advance submission of POSI. If you don't get that, you've wasted your time. Gifts should relate back to your offering and act as a qualifier. *Work backwards from your core offering.* Ask yourself what service your promotion is promoting. Then ask, "What would my prospects need (information, materials, advice) if they needed the promoted service?"

Build your free gift around that need. That gives you an offering that is valuable to both you and your prospect. They will "pay" for the free gift with the POSI you need to begin doing business with them.

Each aspect of your business can and should have its own thought-leadership offer. One size may not fit all. Get your junior staff involved in the writing. You can also use these for SEO optimization.

One mistake I see on LinkedIn are people who write for the sake of generating "content" and "getting their name out there" but not in a way that drives business back to them. That kind of post often comes off as self-serving. On the other hand, posts that provide useful information to an author's target market will drive business. Those posts "do well by doing good." As they are shared and referenced, they help search engines find the provider.

One final note about providing thought leadership as a way of driving POSI: *Keep asking for it.*

"If you found this paper relevant to your business and would like a more personal take on your business issue, we'd like to hear from you. Call John Smith at (204) 891-1891. He'll hear your story and explain how XYZ Company can offer solutions and resolutions."

Discounts:

I have one word of advice for offering to discount a Service in your advertising: Don't.

Even though the call to action in one in five Product ads offered a discount, not a single Service ad offered one. This makes sense, based on what we've already reviewed: Services and Product/Service Hybrids require POSI in order to make a concrete offer with a concrete price.

As a result, it immediately makes Service ads look suspicious when they offer a discount.

"Twenty percent off?" a potential buyer will ask. "Twenty percent off what?"

Buyers understand that it's easy for a seller to inflate a Service quote by 20% to accommodate a 20% "discount." The end result is that the seller looks untrustworthy just as trust is most needed.

It especially doesn't make sense in a B2B environment, where purchases are seldom made impulsively. For an impulse consumer Product, a CTA of "Call before midnight tonight and get 20% off your purchase" might work. But I can't see a city council rushing to define the scope of a billion-dollar bridge project because they want to submit the RFPs before a discount deadline.

For all these reasons, I suggest you don't try to offer a discount on a Service.

That said, Productized Services, as discussed above, can be "discounted" as an incentive, just like Products can. See Rule 10 for more on discounting Productized Services.

Rule Five: Give Away Free Sample Services.

Do Services offer free samples or trials? Can they? Does it make sense for a dentist to offer me a moment or two of free drilling to see if I want to have my fillings done there? Can I get a sense of how well an architect will perform on the overall project by looking at a sketch for one doorway? Free samples are very powerful incentives, and this topic is worth its own section, even though, technically, it falls under the above heading of Free Gifts.

A Closer Look at Sample Services:

As with any Service, a Sample Service requires SI, and so offering a Sample Service directly solicits SI. The agent who wants to sell your business for you gets detailed SI about the business by offering to appraise it for free. Same with the Free Consultation. The consultant gets detailed SI, allowing the firm to quote a price and move toward a sale. None of these samples can be claimed anonymously. Since they are themselves Services, they require at least some of the buyer's service inputs.

Some examples:

- Free Appraisal
- Free Consultation
- First Coding Free
- Free 30-day Trial
- Free Seminar
- Free Starter Kit

Of the 284 Service ads studied, only one contained a CTA offering a trial of some kind.

I was intrigued by this outlier and wondered if anything could be learned from the "exception that proved the rule." After all, even a free trial requires SI from the buyer. If a free-trial model could be generalized, it could prove a powerful tool for gathering POSI early in the buying process.

The free trial came from an insurance coding company. Healthcare providers must code their work in order for insurance companies to pay them. It's time-consuming work, and physicians often outsource it. Healthcare First is a coding agency that makes this offer as part of their CTA:

"Special Offer: Your first coding event is on us."

Why are they able to make an offer of free services?

- Coding is an ongoing series of discrete events. Healthcare providers have to code insurance billing on a continuous and ongoing basis. If the new client is happy with their free trial, then the loss will be recouped.
- It balances the size of the potential loss with the size of the potential gain. Assuming that each coding event is the same size as other coding events, then there is no risk of a huge loss never being recouped.
- Low expertise means low customization. Coders are company-trained hourly workers, not analysts or other creative types.

- Changing providers requires a time investment from the buyer. The buyer can't cherry-pick by coming in for one free event and then disappear. Only a buyer who felt a need for a new supplier would spend the time.
- No outside costs or materials to purchase.

What other business Services meet these criteria and would be suitable examples of free trials?

- Banking plans for professionals or corporations: e.g., initial period with no fees.
- Collection agencies: First $20,000 (or other fixed sum) collected free of charge.
- Group benefits: 30-day coverage free of charge.
- Commission advancement services: First $5,000 (or some other sum) advanced without charge.

In the case of the medical coding, the free service "taste" was exactly the same as the ongoing service it was promoting. But "ongoing" can also refer to different services or different stages of services. For example,

- First checkup free. In fact, most dentists now offer to do a child's first checkup for free.
- Free consultation. Most lawyers offer a "15-minute free consultation."

- Free property appraisal. Doubly powerful because the SI for the free service is exactly the same as the SI for the service the agent is hoping to be paid for later.

Here are examples of businesses that would not meet these criteria:

- Aircraft electronics upgraders (one-time event).
- Architects specializing in artificial ice-skating rinks in shopping malls (one-time event).

These are both one-time events requiring substantial time, materials, and/or thought investment on the part of the service supplier to complete the free event. It would be difficult to recoup that investment.

The key here is that the sample must lead to other business. If a potential client owned hundreds of aircraft, then "first aircraft electronics upgrade" might actually work.

Consider if your business can offer a "free trial" for your business of some kind.

Rule Six: Use a specific contact person in the Call to Action.

Your call to action should refer the buyer to a specific person in your company, and that person should be a technical expert trained in how to collect service inputs during the call.

Rule Six doesn't apply to Products. Anybody can be at the end of toll-free number to ask the two questions relevant for Products:

- Which Product are you ordering today?
- How will you be paying?

They can also be trained to read the brochures and answer Product-feature questions, should any arise in the call.[4]

But the goal of the call to a Service company is different. The Service company wants to get the POSI that will allow them to ultimately make a sale. Therefore, the person answering the phone must be extremely knowledgeable about the Service and able to respond intelligently to any possible scenario that the Service buyer might present.

So who does that person have to be? In my experience, it needs to be the most knowledgeable expert on your team. That is the most senior person, not one of the junior ones.

The offer of expertise, in itself, can be a powerful incentive to a buyer. But for that offer to be believable, it has to prove that the expertise being offered is valid. By naming an "expert," you give credence to the expertise.

When you say, "Call Patty Porteo in our laser design and implementation group at (204) 891-1891," there is an automatic implication that Patty is an expert in laser optics.

While simply naming the expert in the CTA is effective, a short explanation of the credentials is even more effective: "Patty Porteo's papers on the application of lasers to equipment cleaning

---

[4] Twice now I've been in the weird situation where I couldn't find the information I needed from the company's website, so I called their customer service number, and after a few minutes of discussion realized that their CSR was also going through their website looking for the information, retracing the steps I'd just taken.

have been recognized internationally. Patty is part of our laser implementation team and will be happy to discuss your company's challenges. Call today."

Getting the buyer to call is the first half of the equation. The second half is making sure that, when the call comes, the named expert is ready to receive the call. My experience has been that technical experts often need guidance (and sometimes need to be pressured) to become good at answering incoming calls.

Here are the elements of effective call management:

1. A complete list of all Phase One Service Inputs that the company will need to prepare a complete quotation. This checklist means that you won't have to call the prospect back repeatedly to get more information. *Could* the expert do this "on the fly"? Yes. *Should* the expert do this on the fly? No.

2. The expert understands the importance of POSI to the sales process. It can't be something that lip service is paid to.

3. The manner of the person receiving the call should create the expectation that a proposal will be prepared and that the caller will be expected to make a purchase decision based on that proposal. If possible, an appointment to present the proposal should be made during the initial call.

4. A process into which the POSI fits. There should be an automatic and streamlined process that takes the newly acquired POSI to the finished-proposal stage. The expert should not have to think, "Uh, okay, what do I do with this information now?" That process should be pre-defined.

5. There should be a process to identify and rapidly disengage from unqualified buyers to minimize wasted time.

These last two steps ensure that the expert minimizes the time spent on these calls.

Is referring inquiries to a designated expert more effective than referral to an un-named phone number? Well, nine times as many Service ads referred callers to a specific expert compared to Product ads.

It's not just the formal research that suggests that a designated contact is the best way to go. I've seen firsthand how badly the process can go when callers are directed to a general-inquiry call center.

When I was an employee at an international B2B consulting company, the practice heads decided they didn't want to be "bothered" answering random telephone inquiries, at least of half of which came from unqualified buyers. They decided that the junior business-development staff would answer the phones, qualify the callers, and then forward the inquiry up the line.

We received no training, on the assumption that, since we were the business-development people, we'd know what to do.

It was a disaster. For us, for the prospective clients, and for the company.

Simply put, the callers expected us to have very-high-level conversations about every aspect of the company's businesses. Our company had 11 separate practices, and that reflected the fact that sectoral expertise was key in applying our company's offering to the different markets we served. Nobody could be an expert in *all* these areas.[5] Despite our best efforts, we knew we were making the company sound stupid.

We then had the challenge of finding the "right" person to give the lead to. In a global company, that sometimes took a couple of days.

The outcome of the call was that we would take as much information as we thought was needed, and then pass that along to the appropriate managing partner. The most common response was anger and frustration. We'd be asked questions like, "How serious did they sound?" "Why wouldn't they tell you what their budget was?" or "Why didn't you get the XYZ information?"

What was clear was that we had simply added an unnecessary layer to the process, and one of the things that I realized was that it would be easier to train the experts to add a thin layer of sales expertise to their work than to add a thick layer of technical expertise to the salespeople.

Your calls to action should direct buyers to specific company experts, and those experts should be ready for the calls when they come.

Rule Seven: Use intense wording.

Product ads aren't shy about wanting you to take action and buy.

- "Call now!" they scream. "Operators are standing by."
- Limited-time offer.
- Hurry in: Offer valid only while supplies last. No rainchecks!

---

[5] And we were experts in *none* of the areas.

- Independence Day bonus applies only to orders placed before midnight on July 4th.

Product ads get away with this type of promotion because they can state a price and then offer a temporary incentive that increases the perceived value at the stated price point. The discount can take the form of a reduction in price, a free gift with purchase, extra merchandise, or even a free merchandise sample.

It's difficult for amorphous Services to offer the same kind of "deals." But Rules Three through Six change the game by creating an offering that *can* be time limited. Use them to give the buyer a reason to "call now."

- RST Engineering Services is the world leader in Waste Water Management. Is your city's waste-treatment plant having trouble dealing with rising water tables? A summary of RST's research in this area is being published in next month's edition of *Environmental Engineering Magazine*. **RST is making the complete findings of this study available, free of charge, to city engineers until July 20th.** (After July 20th, the full report will be available at our online store for $2,200 plus applicable taxes.) Tell us about your specific challenge, and we'll also share ideas your team can implement to pre-empt problems. Contact Thomas Bear **today** at (204) 891-1891.
- New government regulations come into effect September 1st. Is your team ready? Call us today, and we'll have your systems in place with time to spare.

- Every day you keep using your existing XYZ process, it costs you seven times what you would pay with our RST process. Sandip Sett has helped more than 300 companies like yours make the switch. Call him today.

Rule Eight: Don't reiterate the company's entire value proposition

The most cumbersome Calls to Action were the ones that tried to wrap every aspect of a consulting company's offering into a single call to action. Here are a couple of the, uh, winners from my research:

- *If you have clients with a turnover of more than $100K who would benefit from invoice- and asset-based lending from a solid partner during these turbulent times, call us for an informal chat.*
- *For more information on our consulting services related to compensation, corporate transactions, leadership, talent management, executive compensation, and HR effectiveness, please contact us at companywebsite.*

This last CTA fails on more than one level. Let's deconstruct and improve it:

- Our company has experts who can optimize every aspect of your business.
- For Human Resource Effectiveness issues, including Compensation, contact Xi Lee at (204) 891-1891 ext. 160

- For Leadership and Talent Management issues, including Executive Compensation, contact Judy Jones at (204) 891-1891 ext. 451
- For Corporate Transaction issues, contact Peter Jones at (204) 891-1891 ext. 731

Rule Nine: When to apply what rule.

There is a large body of advertising research that discusses the difference between Search, Experience, and Credence offerings. Dating back to the 1970s, SEC Theory suggests that these three terms can be applied to characterize Products and Services. I think that a more useful way to apply SEC theory is to use it to characterize each *attribute* of an offering, rather than the offering itself:

Search Offerings: Search Offerings can be evaluated prior to purchase. A consumer can look at a pear and know if it's ripe or compare two ads for carpet cleaning to know which has the lowest price per square foot. Note: The term "search" pre-dates the Internet and search engines, so, in this case, the meaning has nothing to do with the offering being "searchable" on the web.

Experience Offerings: Experience Offerings can be evaluated by the purchaser, but only after being consumed. Was the pear as sweet as was hoped? Am I pleased with how the interior designer redecorated my living room?

Credence Offerings: Credence Offerings cannot be evaluated by the buyer even after consumption, and so the buyer must rely on an outside source for evaluation. Did the surgeon put my cardiac stent in the best position possible, or would an extra 2 millimeters further down have been better? Will the brand-new car I just bought remain reliable over the long term? Will my life insurance company pay my death claim after I pay into it for 50 years?

SEC	Definition	Example
Search	Evaluation prior to trial is possible	The pear looks ripe
Experience	Evaluation is possible through trial	The pear was as sweet as I'd hoped
Credence	Evaluation requires outside expertise, even after trial	The pear was high in Vitamin D

Since we can't tell on our own if Credence Offerings are good or not, we rely on third-party evaluations to make purchase decisions, or we rely on other "signals." Signaling is the process in which the provider of a Credence Offering "signals" quality of their offering by surrounding it with tangible items of quality. Some examples?

- Expensive chocolates in a bowl in a luxuriously furnished waiting area.
- Medical-school diplomas prominently displayed on the examination room walls; poster-size reprints of JD Power reliability reports on the showroom walls.
- A large (if seldom used) library of law books clearly visible from the waiting room.
- An expensive pen used for signing contracts that are printed on extra-thick paper and bound in a leatherette cover.

- Clothing/Cars/Watches/Etc. representing brands that an unsuccessful provider would not be able to afford.

Regarding Services marketing, SEC Theory can be combined with Unified Services Theory to make the following observations:

1. Because they have been productized, Productized Services have Search attributes. Potential buyers can compare offers. Advertising should encourage immediate purchase: For example: *Come to Speedy Auto today* for our 10/20 Oil Change—Ten minutes, twenty dollars, and your car is protected.

2. Experience Services should provide an incentive to try a sample of the service (perhaps even a productized version) so that the potential buyer can evaluate the overall service: For example: *"Come try us out!* New customers half price on cut and color. $100 value only $49." When it's not possible to provide a sample of the service, then *many* examples of past work should be provided so the buyer can get a sense of the provider's service outputs. Tattoo parlors have books filled with photos of past work, as do wedding photographers and cosmetic surgeons. Ideally, the example should compare POSI to outcomes. "Our client wanted a round front entryway door. Here's how their house looked when it was finished."

3. Credence Services need some outside confirmation of quality. Publications by employees give credence to the abilities of the service provider while at the same time allowing the

prospective buyer to "try" the approach or thinking of the provider. Simply making white papers available on a website is enough to lend Credence to the author, but publication in a peer-reviewed or subscribed journal is even better. "Lisa Ament's paper on mitigation of non-periodic risks was just published in the *Journal of Consulting Actuaries. Contact her for a copy of the paper and to discuss your challenging risk scenario.*" or "Lisa Ament's landscape designs have won gardening awards across the state."

Make sure you understand your offerings' SEC characteristics and that you are applying the correct promotional approach to each.

Rule Ten: Productized Services.

Once a Service has been productized, it should be advertised the same way as a Product would. The call to action should demand, "Buy Now!" with a click to order and pay. Offer a discount. Since the price of the Productized Service is established, price reductions increase its perceived value. Make sure, however, that *no* service inputs are required. The requirement of any SI means the Productized Service is still a Service.[6]

---

[6] There might seem to be a paradox here, because every online purchase requires the name and address of the buyer. In this case, final selection and payment is being made for the Product, and service inputs (address) are provided for the auxiliary Service (delivery) that makes the overall offering a Service/Product hybrid.

. . . .

Chapter Nine

Advice for Sales Professionals— Everything You Knew About Sales Was At Least a Little Bit Wrong

As discussed in Chapters Five and Six, the sales processes for Services and Products are fundamentally different from one another. We've seen how Products and Productized Services can be sold in a single step, but Services and Product/ Service hybrids always require two steps.

But there are other, very fundamental, sales concepts, such as "The Needs Analysis" and "Features Versus Benefits" that are turned on their heads when moving from Products to Services.

This chapter examines the sales processes for Services. Since this chapter is intended for the Sales team, we'll organize the processes using conventional sales terms:

- Prospecting
- Cold Calling
- Selling Phase One—Capabilities Presentation
- Needs Analysis
- Proposal Writing
- Selling Benefits, not Features
- Selling Phase Two—Pitching
- Closing

Each stage will include sample POSI and PTSI sales scripts to serve as a starting point for your team.

To make sure all readers are on the same page, regardless of their sales training or background, here are some standardized definitions used in this chapter:

- The concept of "sales team" refers to anybody in the company whose job description requires them to find and win business. This could be a dedicated sales department with staff who have titles like "Business Development Manager," or it could be professionals who are working on a Seller/Servicer model and have titles like "Managing Partner."
- The terms "selling" and "personal selling" refer to the conventional selling concept, where a person is trying to drum up business. Personal selling can be for any kind of offering (B2B, B2C, B2P, and so on) and has no boundaries in terms of Products or Services. That is, the offering can be vacuums sold door to door, or custom design and construction of vacuum chambers for industrial metal-plating processes.

- Depending on which "standard" and "classic" and "definitive" sales training manual you favor, there can be anywhere from three to eight steps in the sales process.[1] For example, most companies I've worked with call the pool of prospective buyers their "prospects." Others add a layer and call those companies "suspects," as in "We suspect these people might be interested." They aren't moved to the Prospect pile until the Suspect has somehow confirmed interest.

- Request for Proposal (RFP), Request for Quotation (RFQ), Specifications Document, etc. all refer to a submission of POSI and a request for details and pricing. RFPs can be formal documents, or they can take the form of a casual conversation. Regardless of structure, any submission of POSI from a buyer with a request to prepare a proposal will be termed "RFP."[2]

Let's review some fundamental differences between the sales steps when selling Products versus selling Services, and the relationship between the two processes:

Services have two sales steps:

1. The sale team's goal in the first selling phase is to convince the buyer to submit Phase One Sales Input, that is, the information needed to write a proposal for the buyer.

---

[1] And by the way, whichever theory you happen to like, I probably have a book in my library that contradicts that approach.

[2] Even simple Services require an RFP. When I wanted my quilt cleaned, each cleaner had a list of questions to ask. When I requested a quote (proposal), I had to provide SI in the form of answers to their questions.

Service

Promotion

Customer Gathers Choice Information (Providers)

Customer Provides Service Inputs

Service Quotation

Customer Compares Offers

Final Selection and Payment

Customer Provides Service Inputs

Value Add Phase

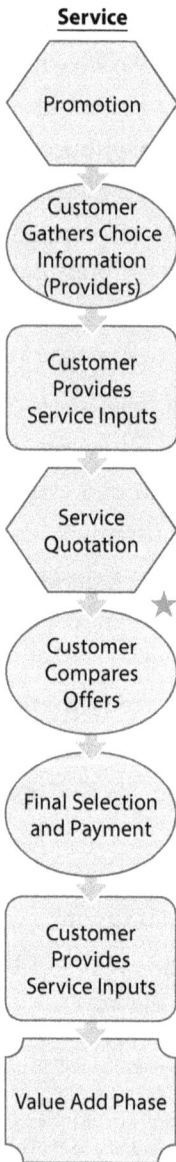

2. In the second step, the proposal is presented to the buyer to be compared to other competing proposals. The sales team's goal in this second sales phase is to convince the buyer to select the company's proposal and make arrangements for payment, thus "making the sale."

A "win" in the first sales presentation means you get here, and a "win" in the second sales presentation means you get here.

Products have one sales step:

1. The buyer makes final selection of the offered Products and provides payment.

Note that a Productized Service is also sold in a single step. The sales team can deliver a complete description, including price, of the Productized Service at the initial meeting, and go on to close the sale at the same meeting.

So, from the point of view of the Service sales team, the second selling phase is exactly like selling a Product.

Chapter Seven offered advice to the Marketing Department on how to create advertising that would cause buyers to send POSI to the

Service

- Promotion
- Customer Gathers Choice Information (Providers)
- Customer Provides Service Inputs
- Service Quotation
- Customer Compares Offers
- Final Selection and Payment
- Customer Provides Service Inputs
- Value Add Phase

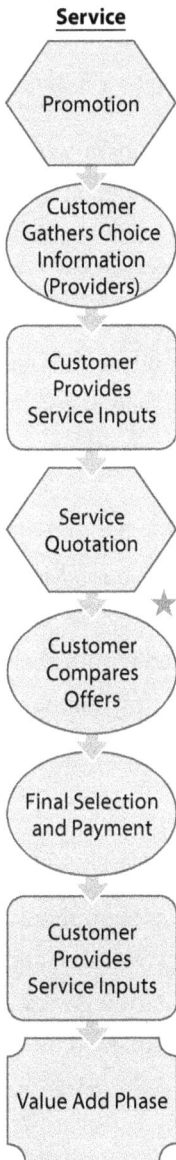

seller. Although most companies don't structure their reporting this way, personal selling is actually part of the marketing process. Cold calling is a form of advertising, and its purpose is to eventually get POSI from the Service buyer.

So what is the sales team "selling" in the first phase? How do we judge if the initial selling phase has been successful?

The goal of the first sale presentation is to convince the buyer to consider your company for future work and to include you in the list of companies to which they send Requests for Proposals. This RFP List can be a formal structure within their department, or it can be a simple mental map that exists in the mind of just one person. In any case, at the end of the presentation, the buyer should have a mental state that says something like, "The next time I need to have XYZ done, I should get a bid from *this* company."

Referring back to the flowchart for selling Services, you can see that the object of the first selling phase is to reach the point of getting the customer to provide Phase One Service Inputs.

Prospecting:

The prospecting phase of Services selling is basically the same as for Product selling. The sales team must compose a list of potential buyers who need and are able to purchase the service. For example:

- Prospective clients for a forensic accounting firm would include: law firms that focus on fraud or personal claims, insurance companies, companies that are in the news because of internal disputes or wrongdoing, etc.
- A landscaper's list of prospective clients would include homeowners who live in nearby neighborhoods with large yards and who have high-enough disposable income to pay for private yard services.

That's Sales 101, and it's *almost* not worth covering here, except for a special consideration that applies to Service companies. Many Service providers term themselves "full-service" agencies. That means that, in their mind, they can fulfill *any* need within their service arena. For example, a full-service engineering company with a thousand employees might have enough internal resources (from architects to tradespeople) to quote on any project, from repairing a bridge to building an apartment complex.

Even full-service agencies, though, have "sweet spots"—things that they can do better than anybody else. The sales team should initiate and lead the discussion to determine their sweet spot and then use that to guide their prospecting phase. Although it's a sales issue, it really cuts to the core of what the company does to earn a profit, and the discussion should include representatives from all areas of senior management.

Early in my relationship as a business-development consultant to a large "general mechanical engineering" firm, I heard them stress that they wanted to bid on "anything." They wanted me to develop a sales team that would call on all large companies, looking for business that spanned their different divisions: Heating-Ventilation-Air-Conditioning (HVAC), factory-equipment repair, factory design and build, commercial-property renovation, and so on. Over the years, they had even come into ownership of restaurants that were in commercial buildings they'd purchased and been the principal contractor for one new housing project. So "anything" was a very wide territory.

When I asked about their ability to *compete and win* in all these areas, they conceded they had trouble competing in most areas. HVAC, for example, was an arena with many competitors and very low margins. In other words, HVAC represented business they were unlikely to win and happy to lose, as it didn't make them much profit.

Instead, I took a close look at the company and determined that the most profitable engagements were with *food packaging* manufacturers, and specifically related to the equipment that made the packaging. We had the expertise to install, customize, and maintain all the specialized subsystems that keep package-making equipment running: high-voltage power distribution, heating and cooling systems, air purification, waste disposal, humidification, etc. We even had a proven track record designing and building new packaging factories.

Here's what you need to know about the package manufacturing: When equipment is running properly, it makes thousands of dollars every hour it operates, but when it's down, it loses thousands of dollars every hour it sits idle. So package-making clients are willing to pay top dollar to ensure it's installed properly, maintained perfectly, and serviced quickly.

This narrowed the prospect list from "everybody and everything" to a few hundred food processors and package-manufacturing companies. We were able to narrow the field further by eliminating the companies that couldn't afford "best in class" services and so got rid of the small companies and the ones that were struggling. The final list of about 100 large and growing companies represented our "real" prospects, that is, companies that needed our unique area of expertise (food-packaging-equipment repair) and that were able to pay top dollar for a specialized service.

When cold calling with the focused message that "we repair and maintain package-making equipment," almost every prospect wanted to meet with us to hear about our capabilities. Most importantly, it was the perfect door opener. In the statement of capabilities, we made the point that we could design and build an entire packaging factory as a turnkey design/build project for them, and that led the prospects to ask about other work, like HVAC repairs to their existing facilities.

Sales and Marketing teams at full-service companies should lead the charge to find an area of focus to leverage as a door opener, even when the company as a whole is looking for a broader reach.

One international sales manager I've worked with used this term: "pre-needs-analysis needs analysis." He explained that his group met before approaching a prospect and tried to figure out what the prospect needed. Then they would know what aspect of their offering they should open the conversation with.

Cold Calling:[3]

When a Product salesperson calls on a prospective buyer, there's something to talk about. Let's look at the case of a supplier of raw materials, such as chicken to a restaurant or plastic to an injection-molding company: In both those cases, it's easy for the salesperson to state a purpose for a call:

- Our company offers XYZ Product.
- We'd like you to consider buying *our* brand of Product.
- I'd like to set a time to show you our Product catalogue, explain pricing, and detail our competitive advantage over other suppliers.

When a Service salesperson calls, there are problems when using a similar script:

- Our company offers XYZ Services.
- We'd like you to consider *us* as a Service provider.
- I'd like to set a time to show you our
  - ~~Service catalogue~~, (There is no Service catalogue. Services are created to fill the needs of the buyer in an ad hoc fashion.)
  - ~~explain pricing~~, (No pricing without POSI)

---

[3] Cold calling can be by telephone, email, in person, etc.

- ~~and detail our competitive advantage over other suppliers~~
(As discussed in Chapter Two, it's very difficult to differentiate between two full-service firms.)

So what *should* the outline of a Service cold call look like?
Well, it *could* look like this:

1. Our company offers XYZ services.
2. We'd like you to consider us as a service provider.
3. I'd like to set a time to deliver a statement of capabilities
   and demonstrate what we can do for your company.

In this case, the term "capabilities presentation" takes the place
of "sales presentation." It recognizes that you have nothing to sell
to them but want to talk about the scope of your work.

There are a couple of problems with this approach. First of all,
it's hard to know what any client needs at a given moment in time,
so it's hard to know "what you can do for them." Secondly, your
goal is to get information (POSI), and this approach is structured
around an offer to give them information. While you can hope
that talking about your services will elicit a similar exchange of
information (that is, an RFP), it doesn't "get them talking," and it's
easy for them to decline your offer of a meeting. Here's a variation:

1. Our company offers XYZ services.
2. We'd like you to consider us as a service provider.
3. I'm calling to find out what your process is for considering new suppliers. Some companies have new-vendor

fairs, some have a formal vetting process through their procurement department, and, in some cases, it's just a matter of meeting with the department to offer a short statement of capabilities. What is the best way for us to introduce ourselves?

This approach completely changes the game. Almost the very first thing you do is to start asking them for information about their work. That act breaks their concentration, and it's not a "yes/no" question, so they can't just answer, "No, we don't want to meet." In the thousands of times I've done this on behalf of large and small service providers, I can count on one hand the number of times that a prospective buyer has refused to answer. The answers varied but always paved the way for the next step.

The most frequent answer was that they wanted us to present to them:

"Well, usually, we would set up a face-to-face introductory meeting of some kind with our whole team so that we could learn about your work. That way, we can ask for details about the things that are more interesting for us."

An opening big enough to drive a truck through.

Here's another example of using the "get information instead of giving information" approach:

1. Our company offers XYZ services.
2. We'd like you to consider us as a service provider.

3. The article in last month's *International Journal of Your Field* mentioned that you were looking at reducing costs across the board on your XYZ. We have a unique approach to XYZ that might benefit your team. How would we go about sharing the details?

Whatever your door-opening question is, remember these two principles:

- Not a yes-or-no question. You are asking them about their process.
- Your question can't require a non-disclosure agreement to hear the answer. For example, you could not change the last example to "The article in last month's *International Journal of Your Field* mentioned that you were looking at reducing costs across the board on your XYZ. What have you done to reduce the costs of your XYZ?"

That question asks a stranger about their competitive strategies. It might work as an opener at a very small company or in B2C selling, but my experience is that most buyers at big companies are *trained* to refuse to answer. At this point in your relationship with the prospective client, they don't know who you are (you could even be a competitor), and those questions are none of your business.[4]

---

[4] Hi, Apple? Our company tests graphic user interfaces on portable electronics, and we'd like to be considered as a provider of services. Could you tell me all about your next round of innovation for the iPhone iOS? Hello? Hello?

Getting Ready for the Statement of Capabilities

In the time approaching that first Statement of Capabilities (SOC), you can play the detective to find out what they might be interested in. If they use Outlook to schedule the meeting, you can see who is coming from their team. A visit to LinkedIn will tell you what areas those people are responsible for. I've even called them in advance of the meeting to introduce myself.

> "Hi, John. My name is David Selch, and I'm part of the team from XYZ company that's going to be presenting to your team on the 15th. This is really just a courtesy call. We want to make sure we are showing our most relevant work, and I just wanted to make sure you're still working on MNOP and EFG."

The obvious reason for doing this is to make sure that your SOC focuses on the right areas of your offering, but there is a second, more strategic, reason: Every bit of information you find constitutes service inputs, as it gives you deep background to future RFPs.

In the days leading up to the meeting, I forward a short agenda that *makes clear we have an expectation of receiving SI* from the client:

Hi, Alishiah,

Looking forward to seeing you next week. Our agenda is pretty straightforward. Basically we're going to talk about our work but also give your team the chance to talk about your work as well. Here's our plan:

- 10–12 minutes: Basic introductions—I'll introduce our three speakers and give the one-minute summaries of their work. If you could then introduce the members of your team and give an overview of their work, I'd appreciate it. I'll also give the 20,000-foot view of our company.
- 8 Minutes: Susan Yoon, expert in ABC techniques, will talk about our ABC caps.
- 8 Minutes: John Smith will explain our DEF approach.
- 8 Minutes: Ahmed Abboud: Case study using GHI to reduce costs of JKL.
- 8 Minutes: Opportunity for your team to talk about upcoming projects and ask our team about specific experience with that type of work.
- Balance of time: Questions and Answers, and/or Case Studies supporting the previous step.

We are looking forward to seeing you. If there are any changes to this proposed agenda that would make our time together more useful to you, we are open to suggestions. If you'd like to forward an NDA in advance of the meeting, I'll make sure our Legal folks have signed off prior to our arrival.

David

There's an old sales maxim that "Telling is not Selling," and this is literally true with Services. If you aren't getting SI, then you're not selling, so every interaction with the client needs to be geared to this.

The Phase One Sales Presentation, aka The Statement of Capabilities:

As was just demonstrated with the agenda for the meeting, the presentation of capabilities has four major parts:

1. Overview and introductions
2. Details of capabilities, approaches, experience, expertise, etc. that your pre-needs-analysis needs analysis indicates are most relevant
3. Solicitation of RFPs or other service input
4. Creation of expectation of future follow-up to discuss future SI

I'll assume that your company is already pretty good at explaining points one and two. There are plenty of articles on the Internet regarding "elevator scripts" and how to present. Let's look at a couple of examples for ways to ask for SI:

"Could you bring a calendar showing the projects you will have to execute over the next 6–9 months? Then we can get a sense of where our work might dovetail with yours."

"We've read in industry newsletters that you will be focusing on changing the XYZ in your ABC product range. We'd like an opportunity to bid on those projects. What is your process for sharing RFPs? Is there a list we have to get on? Actually, if you could give us an idea of what your next few projects will look like, we can let you know where you should be including us with an RFP."

The trick is to ask about all their work but to be clear you are going to reject the areas where other vendors could do a better job than you. Pick a subset, and ask the client to include you in the RFP list.

"Honestly, those first two are areas where we can do a good job, but it's not our main focus. If you have solid relationships with providers in those areas, we wouldn't want to disturb them. On the other hand, the last two you mentioned are right in our wheelhouse, and I can bring expertise and efficiencies that make us our clients' first choice for that type of work. We'd very much like to write a proposal for those two. Can we keep in touch regarding the details?"

How do you measure success for the first meeting? If, as an outcome of your presentation, the client sends you RFPs, then the meeting was a success. The sooner the first RFP arrives, the more successful the presentation. If the RFPs are high quality, it was more successful yet.

If you get an RFP two years later for something you don't really do? Not so successful.

While you will want to get an RFP during the meeting, or at least the promise from the client to immediately send POSI after the meeting, the reality is that's not always possible. Some services are purchased on an ongoing basis, producing a steady

Service

- Promotion
- Customer Gathers Choice Information (Providers)
- Customer Provides Service Inputs
- Service Quotation
- Customer Compares Offers
- Final Selection and Payment
- Customer Provides Service Inputs
- Value Add Phase

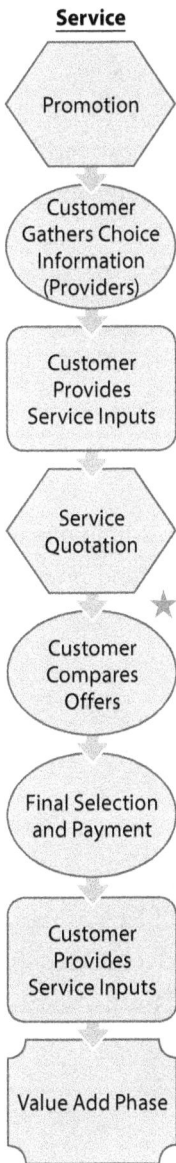

stream of RFPs; other are purchased sporadically, perhaps only once or twice a year. If your industry is more like the former, it is perfectly acceptable to evaluate yourself with the question, "Did I leave with an RFP?" If the latter, then you need to ask yourself the question, "How will I stay in contact with this client over the next few months so we are top of mind when they need to buy?"

You are trying to get to here.

When designing your follow-up strategy, you should consider using a POSI "proxy." The term "proxy" refers to information that takes the place of actual service inputs. Proxies allow you to write a proposal without needing to receive the "more difficult to transport" service inputs of person or property. Even a description of a large dataset, rather than the dataset itself, can simplify proposal writing.

For example, an accountant will eventually need to receive all of a company's financial information, but in order to quote a price needs to know only certain placeholder (proxy) information. This would include such facts as the number of employees, the type of record-keeping system used by the client, and so on.

Your sales team should decide if a proxy is sufficient to provide a service quotation. If there is no proxy to use, then you must determine an acquisition strategy for POSI *before* your SOC.

Look twice before giving up on the idea of a proxy, even if you have to invent one. An investment in a proxy system can provide a competitive edge that makes your offering more "buy-able" in a crowded market.

For example, anilox rollers, used in commercial presses, weigh hundreds of pounds. A company that provides an anilox roller cleaning service should consider finding a proxy so that the actual rollers don't have to be moved just to provide a quotation.

Instead of this:

We'll courier you a special wooden crate so you can ship one of your anilox rollers to us. Our team will examine it and provide a quote for cleaning.

Try this:

We'll have a team come out and examine your anilox rollers so we can provide a quote for cleaning.

Or this:

We'll send you a handheld spectrometer that will let you measure the dirt levels on your anilox rollers yourselves. Once we have a couple of measurements and the number of rollers, we can provide a quote for cleaning.

Conversely, there are situations when you will strategically choose not to accept a proxy, in order to increase personal contact with a newer client:

Use of Proxy:

"We'll watch for a final copy of your floor plans in about two months. If we don't see them in, say, eight weeks, I'll check back with you. Once we have the floor plans, we can work on the furnishing designs and send a design board and some preliminary pricing."

Avoidance of Proxy:

"We'll plan on coming back to see you in about two months once you have your final floor plans. We can sit down together with a few of our design boards and get a sense of your tastes in fabrics and colors, and we'll take the information we need to do some preliminary pricing."

Your sales team has to understand, *before* the initial statement of capabilities:

- Is it possible to leave with an RFP?
- If so, how do we structure the SOC to ensure that outcome?
- If not, how do we structure the SOC to create expectation for later follow-up?
- Who is responsible for follow-up?[5]
- What form should that follow-up take? Proxy? Non-Proxy?

---

[5] When a team of business developers and technical experts co-present a statement of capabilities, they should know who is responsible for follow-up after the meeting. I once had a client ask, "Who should we send the RFP to?" and four people on my team simultaneously answered, "Me."

The Needs Analysis—Convergent versus Divergent Selling:

When a patient visits a doctor with a problem, the doctor uses a process that physicians call "differential diagnosis." The doctor asks a series of questions, each of which narrows down the field of possible problems, allowing the doctor to make a final diagnosis.

What brings you in today? (At this point, the diagnosis could be anything from a broken toe to erectile dysfunction.)

I'm not feeling well. (We remove things like "broken bones" from the possible diagnosis. At this point, the diagnosis could be anything from a cold to colon cancer.)

What seems to be the trouble?

Well, my head hurts all the time. (So not colon cancer, but maybe high blood pressure, migraine, concussion, a need for eyeglasses, or just too much coffee.)

Is it a sharp pain or a dull pain? The whole head or just part? How long has this been going on? What time of day does this start? Let's take your blood pressure. Can you read this eye chart? (Each question and test narrows the list of potential problems.)

Each question *differentiates* one condition from another. Eventually, the doctor is able to make a diagnosis. Only one condition meets all of the criteria, and the physician knows what the patient "needs" to get better. Then the doctor can prescribe a solution.[6]

---

[6] True story: I had a situation where the doctor told me on a Friday that my dizziness was caused by one of two things: Either an inflammation in my inner ear, which could be resolved by an antihistamine pill, or by an inoperable and fast-growing brain tumor which would certainly kill me within 90 days. One or the other. He was sending me for a CT scan (first thing Monday) to determine which, but in the meantime was prescribing the antihistamine.

The sales process can be summarized as "prove the need, create desire, pre-empt objections." For this first step, salespeople are trained to conduct a "needs analysis," which is analogous to Medicine's differential diagnosis.

Here is a simple example:

A car salesperson greets a couple on the showroom floor and starts asking questions about the kind of car they need: How many passengers? Will they be towing a trailer? Would a sunroof be worth the extra expense? and so on. In this way, a salesperson can "prescribe" the couple an appropriate vehicle, whether that's a 7-passenger van with a larger engine and factory-installed trailer hitch, or a two-seater convertible.

In both the needs analysis and differential diagnosis, a winnowing process systematically limits the solution set. The ultimate goal is to *converge* on a single answer. Once the salesperson has helped the buyer make a final selection, the only other step is to convince the buyer to make payment. Final selection of product and payment are the two steps of a Product sale.[7]

For a Product salesperson, the field of possible solutions is made up of the company's product offerings, or a combination of products. You would not, for example, expect a car salesperson to point out that taking a taxi would offer better value, or a Ford salesperson to tell you that Honda makes exactly what you need. Part of a good salesperson's job (and I'm not singling out

---

[7] If you ever want to drive a car salesperson crazy, explain that you can't see a difference between the 7-passenger van and the extended-seating SUV. Until you do, the salesperson can't go on to try to close you. They can't take offers on two cars at once. They *need* convergence.

car dealers here) is to gently shoehorn the buyer into a solution composed of the salesperson's product line.

The Product needs analysis is therefore a *convergent* process. The solution set converges on a single "best" offering for the customer's needs.

When a Product salesperson's needs analysis receives more information, it results in a finer convergence within the Product-solution set. For example, once settling on a KIA Soul with manual transmission, the salesperson will ask for more information about the customer's preferences regarding air conditioning and color.

When needs analyses are done by multiple vendors offering competing Products, the needs analyses converge on comparable products from different providers. In fact in the automotive world, competitors speak of classes of vehicles: subcompact, SUV, cross-over, family van, and so on. These classes represent competing endpoints to the needs analysis.

Services are completely different. A Service, by definition, is customized based on the client's needed outcomes. The solution set, therefore, *diverges* according to service inputs. The questions in a needs analysis aren't meant to limit an existing set of standard offers. Instead, questions better inform the ultimate design of the service.

This divergence results in:

- Large differences between solutions proposed by different service providers for an individual client's specific situation
- Large differences between solutions proposed by one service provider for different clients

Let's look at a fictional example:

A global company that manufactures office printers and photo-copiers knows that the ongoing cost of toner is of greater concern to buyers than the initial capital cost of the machine itself. They are considering a new offer, called The Infinity Printer, where buyers get a free lifetime supply of toner. When The Infinity Printer is running low, it automatically orders a new toner cartridge from the local supplier.

Of course, the initial cost of The Infinity Printer will be very high compared to the normal offering, but it is a safe bet for the buyer, who knows in advance the overall cost of ownership. The manufacturer has a price point in mind for The Infinity Printer that will earn the company the same profit as they would have earned with a more conventional offering.

The question is, "How much are buyers willing to pay for The Infinity Printer?"

The company decides to hire a professional market-research firm to get a meaningful answer. They issue an RFP explaining the situation and asking for proposals that detail the methodol-ogy and costs for the project. Seven companies respond with proposals that differ wildly in scope and cost:

Company A: Focus groups with SOHO business owners, eight participants in each of four American cities

Company B: In-depth phone interviews with 10 key opinion leaders in the printing industry

Company C: Survey and discussion in an online community composed of salespeople working in the printer aisles at Best Buy and Staples

Company D: Survey emailed out to 3000 owners of printers who have registered their email addresses as part of the warranty registration process

Company E: Experimentation in store. An existing regular printer is mocked up with signage announcing it as *The Infinity Printer* to see if people select the product when it appears to be available. The price is slowly increased to see at what point people stop choosing it. (During the experiment, should a buyer try to purchase the non-existent product, their disappointment is mitigated with a big discount on the corresponding actual printer along with some free toner cartridges.)

Company F: Experimentation in an online virtual-reality store. Exactly as in E, except shoppers are viewing virtual 3-D products on display in a virtual 3-D store on the Internet

Company G: Examines 10 years of store-receipt data to determine the behavior of printer buyers based on feature sets and cost of toner cartridges over time to build a predictive model and then use *The Infinity Printer's* proposed characteristics to draw sales-volume figures at different price points.

As you can see, the only thing these proposals have in common is that they will answer the business question. Each solution diverges from the other *completely*.

Now imagine that each market research firm's salesperson—as part of a needs analysis—asks the question, "What country or countries are you thinking about selling *The Infinity Printer* in?" The answer comes back, "Germany, UK, USA, and India."

The additional detail (about national markets) does not make the proposals converge; it simply fine-tunes the details of the divergence.

Company A decides it needs 30 focus groups in 4 countries, not 4 focus groups in 1 country. They add translations services and travel costs into their proposal.

Company G changes their model to include receipt data from all 4 countries. They hire an outside firm to provide data on India, where they have no access to data. They also hire an economist to adjust the pricing model to take into account SOHO buying power and incomes in each of the 4 countries.

Company F opens the virtual-store experience to participants from around the world, bragging that they will be able to speak to dozens of countries, not just four, and so on.

Notice that, as additional POSI was provided by the client, the new information didn't cause small changes to the proposals. It forced major changes to structure or direction: a new expert economist, engagement of an outside firm, and a focus on the competitive advantage of Company F. As more information was uncovered in the needs analysis, the proposals diverged further.

- When a Product salesperson conducts a needs analysis, the information is used to *converge* on a product mix offer that will meet those needs.

- When a Service salesperson conducts a needs analysis, the information is used to create an offer that *diverges* from other offers.

If the Product salesperson's needs analysis is successful, then the Product salesperson has essentially helped the buyer make a *final product selection,* and the salesperson can, in that same initial meeting, go on to a "close," that is, try to convince the buyer to *provide payment* for that selection.

On the other hand, the Service salesperson's needs analysis, even if successful, accomplishes only the goal of the first sales process, namely acquisition of Phase One Service Inputs. The salesperson then has to take that POSI back to develop the offer. The Service sales process requires two steps—one step to gather POSI, and the second to present the proposal.

Writing the Proposal:

I'm going to assume at this point that your company is flourishing because you know how to write a winning proposal for your industry. There are only three points I'll make here:

Prepare an all-inclusive list of POSI you need to write proposals. That way, you can efficiently get those specifications from the client in a single communication. I've seen many novice salespeople have to call back repeatedly to get "one more thing" from the client.

Don't make assumptions about what they will or won't like or need. **Ask the client,** especially if you are making assumptions that affect a competitive advantage. If your proposal makes a big deal about including an XYZ as part of the project (because you're the world leader in XYZ), and the client already owns your competitor's XYZ, then your proposal will fall flat. In that case, you'd do better to brag about your ability to integrate your solution with your client's XYZ, rather than offer to sell them something they already have. This is a time when it's worth communicating with the client to ask questions. As with the previous point, try to bundle your questions, rather than continuously interrupt the client.

Understand how the current service fits into the client's ongoing plans. What related services were already purchased? How will the finished output of your service be used in the future? If you don't understand the bigger picture, your landscaping quotation could detail the beautiful (and expensively planted) garden they asked for... right where they plan to put a swimming pool next year.

Having more information than your competitors at the proposal-writing phase is a secret weapon. It lets your experts make suggestions to improve your offering. Let's say the RFP calls for rebuilding one piece of equipment in their 17-piece assembly line. If you are the only vendor that knows there are four other pieces of equipment that need rebuilding, and you suggest they do all five pieces at once, it means reducing their shut-down time by 80%—a huge savings for them. Even if they don't want to do it that way (or can't afford to), it shows you are "smarter" than your competitors.

If your proposal is the only one that integrates "current" into "ongoing," you have a powerful competitive advantage.

The Phase Two Sales Presentation, aka The Proposal:

As discussed in Chapter Six, the Service proposal is essentially the "product" you are selling. All of the techniques of "regular" Product selling now apply to your Service. Here the best practices for selling the proposal.

Don't just *send* your proposal to the client—*present* your proposal to the client. In person, via WebEx, or even in a phone call, whenever possible, walk your client through the presentation. Many professionals (the key component in many Service offerings) are uncomfortable wearing the "salesperson" hat. They would rather simply email the proposal to the client and hope for the best. It's far more powerful to walk the client through it, ideally in person (but through a remote presentation, if need be). In that presentation, you will *show the client the features* in your offering and *explain their benefits*.

When a Product salesperson makes a sales presentation, they highlight the features of their product and explain why those features make their brand better than their competitors' offering. A Service salesperson delivering a Service proposal is indistinguishable from a Product salesperson delivering a Product proposal. Your proposal has unique features and provides unique benefits compared to your competitors' proposals. Take the time to "sell" your proposal by walking the buyer through the proposal. Don't assume that the buyer will recognize every advantage in your proposal.[8]

---

[8] In theory, the role of the buyer is to pay perfect attention to each proposal and to pick the optimum solution. In reality, buyers are human beings experiencing distractions. Help them to do the right thing (that is, to choose *your* proposal).

Not all clients will allow you to present your proposal, but when they do, it's a powerful process, for several reasons: You differentiate yourself from competitors who "hit send and pray," the client gets to ask questions without delay, and personal communication is warmer. Most importantly, though, it gives you a chance to adapt your proposal to changing conditions.

There is a fundamental rule in Services Science called *The Principle of Unreliable Customer Inputs.* In a Service process, customer service inputs are *the* key raw materials in your value-add process. Basically, this principle reminds you that sometimes, clients

   a. Change their minds
   b. Don't know what they're talking about
   c. Don't understand what they need
   d. Aren't good communicators[9]

The parameters of a project can change at any time, including *after* you've finished and delivered your proposal. By presenting your proposal, rather than just sending it off, you have the opportunity to update and re-propose.

Once your proposal has been delivered, check back with the client to make sure that the parameters of the project haven't changed. Even though it's fair to expect that a client would contact you to tell you if this was the case, in reality, it doesn't always happen that way. In reality, the client may get busy and find time to give the updates to just some of the vendors that submitted

---

[9] Sadly, these are not mutually exclusive.

proposals. So even if you have the cleverest approach and the lowest price for equipping 50 dentists with mobile treatment vans, if the client now realizes they need 100 mobile pediatric clinics designed instead, your proposal is worthless.

Here is how to professionally follow up on a proposal:

The day after sending, telephone to follow up. Leave a voicemail if need be. Calling is the preferred mode because part of what you are doing is to make sure that the proposal didn't end up in a spam folder. I am stunned by the many times the proposal didn't get to where it was intended to go.[10]

> "I'm calling to make sure you received the proposal, and to see if you had any early feedback. Did we address all your needs?"

The wrong way to contact the client is to call "to touch base."

> "Hi, John—it's David. Hadn't heard from you in a while so I thought I'd just touch base…"

Be specific in your call:

> "Hi, John. I'm calling to reiterate our interest in working with you and to see if there are any changes we could make to the proposal to make it more useful for you."

---

[10] The commission rate on proposals that end up in the spam folder is zero.

In this case, the use of the phrase "more useful" is completely open-ended and opens the door to anything the client needs to move the buying decision forward. The client could ask for a change in any parameter, including price, and this is often where a price negotiation starts.

In fact, in conventional selling terminology, this is what is called a "trial close." You check to see if the customer is ready to buy, and if he is not, try to adapt your offer.

Here are some of the responses I've actually received with this approach:

- I'm glad you called. My boss made some changes, and I was able to reach only a couple of the companies that had submitted bids.
- I really liked your proposal. The problem is that our corporate rules allow me to approve projects up to only $99,999. Your quote is for $105,000. That means I have to wait until next week's meeting to present it for group approval. If you can reduce the price to 99K, I can approve it right now.
- We thought your assumption of XYZ would not be enough to accomplish the goals of the project. Can you explain why your XYZ was so low and maybe requote with more XYZ?
- Is there a way to push the delivery date closer? We need it sooner than we thought.
- You were the only bidder to suggest 500 XYZs. The other four bidders all quoted on either 300 or 200. Could you come back with quotes on 200 and 300?

Keep in mind that *in none of these situations did the client call me.* Nobody reached out to ask for a change of count, to ask a question, or to see if I could move the start date up. Since these were all projects that the client viewed as "required," I am assuming that they called some of the vendors for a re-quote, but not me.

Features and Benefits:

Salespeople are taught that it's a mistake just to list a product's *features* during the sales presentation. A more powerful approach is to point out the *benefits* of the features in the same breath the feature is mentioned. Here's a snippet of conversation you might overhear at a car dealership:

Salesperson	Let me show you the engine.
Buyer	I don't really know about car engines.
Salesperson	Well, let's take a look. As you can see, there are flared air intakes here and here, which means the fuel injectors can work more efficiently, and you get better mileage. Is good mileage important to you?
Buyer	Yes.
Salesperson	Notice the width of the sway bar.
Buyer	The what now?
Salesperson	The bar across the top is called a sway bar. Most cars in this class don't have one. The sway bar means your car will steer more accurately, allowing you to avoid collisions, even at high speeds. Will you be carrying your family on highway trips?

Buyer	Yes.
Salesperson	Are you concerned for their safety?
Buyer	Yes.
Salesperson	So between the sway bar and the flared intakes, you have a car that's going to get great mileage in the city and be super safe on the highway.

Flared intakes and a wide *sway bar* are features. *Great mileage* and *safety on the highway* are the *benefits* that drive the purchase of the vehicle. A Product's benefits are chosen prior to its design, and then baked into the Product when it's made. The manufacturer adds value long before the buyer-seller interaction. As a result, the salesperson has features and benefits to brag about during the sales presentation.

Let's compare this to conversation at a tailor's shop:

Salesperson	Can you tell me what you're looking for in a suit? Cut, buttons, etc.?
Buyer	Well I'm pretty conservative. I need something that's not too flashy. Something that I can wear in a variety of situations.
Salesperson	Where would you be wearing the suit? Day to day? Special events?
Buyer	Well, I work in an office, but it's pretty much Casual Friday every day. I wear chinos and a sports shirt, and sometimes a blazer over that. But when I see clients, I have to wear a suit. And I need to look successful. The clients don't see me

very often, so I can get by with just a couple of suits as long as I mix up the shirts and ties. I'm looking for something "unmemorable" in terms of fabric, so that I don't run into the situation where they remember my outfit and think to themselves, "Hmm… he wore that same suit the last two times he was here."

Salesperson Okay. So classic cut and basic solid colors that you can wear with anything.

In this case, the buyer states the ultimate purchase benefits that he would like to enjoy from the service provider: *a suit that is unmemorable, but successful looking.* The salesperson (the tailor) works backwards from those benefits to define a series of features that will produce those benefits: *classic cut* and *basic solid colors that can be worn with anything.* The features are defined as part of the seller-buyer interaction, and the value is added after the Service is purchased.

Did you notice the difference in who was doing the talking?

In the 143-word conversation at the dealership, the Product salesperson spoke 130 words, and the customer spoke only 13 words. More than 90% of the conversation was the salesperson talking.

In the 170-word conversation at the tailor, the Service salesperson spoke only 40 words, and the customer 130 words. More than three-quarters of the conversation was the customer talking.

We often think of a good salesperson as a "fast talker," somebody who can keep spouting features and benefits even when a customer appears uninterested, hoping that one of the benefits will hit a Hot Button that can become the basis of a close. To sell Services, a salesperson must be a good listener. The more information the salesperson receives, the better the provider team can fine-tune the offering. When I think of an idealized Services salesperson, I think of the caricature of Sigmund Freud asking, "Tell me more about your mother."

Closing:

My experience with professional services is that professionals put a huge effort into preparing a proposal but then do little or nothing to follow up once it's sent. They have the perception that "I gave it my best shot, so it's out of my hands." This isn't true. It's a mistake to assume that the client is not susceptible to persuasion, if that persuasion is delivered in a professional manner. In the seller/servicer model ("eat what you kill"), the professional team *is* the salesperson, and that team needs basic sales training if they are going to build their practice. On the other hand, if a salesperson is representing the professional, then they must be knowledgeable enough about the firm's services to negotiate terms without the help of the experts that will actually provide the service.

Your Service proposal is a de facto Product that you are offering to sell to your client. Like any other Product, it has set parameters, delivery conditions, and a set price. The contract is a purchase agreement. By signing on the dotted line, the client is making the final selection and need only make payment for the purchase.

As a result, *all of the traditional closing techniques that apply to Products apply to your Service as well.* True, some modifications may need to be made, but let's look at some examples using some of Brian Tracy's methods. If you haven't read Brian Tracy's *24 Techniques for Closing the Sale*[11], you should know that the timeless classic is available free of charge from his website: www.BrianTracy.com. Look on the homepage for links to free resources.

Many of Tracy's approaches are immediately applicable to Services, and others can be adapted for Services by keeping in mind that Services are processes that utilize time—of humans and of machines. *Product closing techniques are based on leveraging feature limitations* ("We're almost out of the red ones"), and *Service closing techniques are based on leveraging time limitations.*

As an example, I'll create some Service variations of Brian Tracy's "Last One" close:

---

[11] Brian Tracy is offering a verbatim transcript of a training tape I grudgingly paid money for more than 30 years ago. It was the first sales training material I ever bought, and it's paid for itself a thousandfold and made me a believer in sales training. For most salespeople, *24 Techniques* is the starting point of their sales training and success. I've made every salesperson who has ever worked for me listen to this video. If you are a professional offering an optional service (e.g., a cosmetic surgeon rather than a cardiovascular surgeon), you should download the booklet. Incredibly, it's free. *Free is my favorite price.*

- Dr. Chan has only two surgery dates available before he leaves for the summer. You should take one before they're gone. (Limitation of human time)
- I can guarantee the completion dates assuming the machine is not being used for another project. Once somebody else books it, we can't process your work until that work is done. Is there any reason you wouldn't want to book your work now? (Limitation of machine time)
- Anything that's not in by October 31 isn't going to get done this year. Once November rolls around, we'll be booked solid until February. (Limitation of human time)

Should you offer a discount to close?

Earlier in the book, I said that you should not offer a discount as a way of increasing POSI because Services have no set price. If you offer 15% off, the client will surely ask, "15% off what?" At that point in the selling process, discounting is meaningless. However, your proposal *does* have a set price, and that frames its value. Discounting price increases value. As with any Product discount, you need to have a reason to discount.[12]

---

[12] It doesn't have to be a *good* reason, but it must be *some* reason. That's why car dealerships will have Halloween Sales. If you don't have an excuse for discounting, it begs the question, "*Why is the regular price so high?*" Hence excuses like, "We left the mattress-making machine on all weekend and have to clear them out before the boss gets back from vacation."

Here are two examples:

- I'm paying workers who are sitting idle right now who are scheduled to start other projects in 16 days. If we could kick off tomorrow, I can use them and offer you a discount.
- The price is guaranteed for 23 days. After that, we have to requote because our suppliers have told us the price of cement will definitely be increasing, so you can basically save 4–5% by buying now.

These closing techniques will work in situations in which the buyer is actually able to make a buying decision if given a good reason to do so. If a committee has to have 15 meetings over six months to jointly sign off on a $500 million project, then "closing techniques" won't work. What will work is systematically re-tweaking your offer. The sales team has to keep the channel of communication open over those six months to repeatedly ask, *How can we make our proposal more useful to you?* Don't just repeatedly "touch base" to "see if they have any questions."

You might wonder if the "offering to make changes to the proposal" would be equally useful for selling Products. I don't believe so. The optimization process for Products occurs during the design phase of the product or product line, before it's even manufactured. The needs analysis uncovers which variation is the best solution for a given buyer. If there were other variations available, they should have been part of the converging process.

Isn't it interesting that the nature of the needs analysis at the *beginning* of the selling process affects which closing techniques can be used at the *end* of the process?[13]

Every point in the sales process from Prospecting to Closing is different when comparing Products and Services. It's important that every member of the Sales team understands how to optimize each step. If you are a one-person-shop, it's easy to make sure you are implementing each stage properly. In a large sales team, where there are inside salespeople setting appointments for outside salespeople doing statements of capabilities who must then coordinate with technical experts to create a proposal, you have to make sure that everybody knows their job. Moreover, you have to make sure that each person knows the job of the others in the group so they can integrate and optimize. You don't want your opportunities to get "eaten by the machine."

---

[13] What is the best way to close a Product sale? I have no idea. I've spent the last 25 years selling Services. Perhaps there is a book somewhere entitled *Product Reboot*.

Chapter Ten

Notes for Human Resources—Care and Feeding of Your Services Salesperson

A s discussed in Chapter Five, the vast majority of sales hires don't work out, even when they have been successful in other sales roles. This observation applies to both Service and Product offerings. I believe the reason there is such a poor result in sales recruitment is that Human Resource Managers have been making good decisions based on bad information about the nature of selling and what makes a salesperson successful.

There is currently a trend in sales recruiting to focus on two related fallacies: *a good salesperson can sell anything* and *past performance is the key indicator of future performance*. A belief in these axioms can be seen in job postings that say, "Please do not apply if you have not surpassed your sales budget in at least 12 of the last 16 quarters."

Prior to the publication of UST, it was impossible to see that "sales" wasn't a homogeneous process and that there were two different skill sets needed for success in selling Products versus Services.

We don't say, "A remarkable athlete can excel at any sport." That's because we can immediately see that different sports require different abilities and tendencies. A world-class Sumo wrestler would have trouble migrating to a professional basketball career. But even beyond the obvious physical requirements, there are personality characteristics that matter. High Jumping and Golf are solitary pursuits requiring an ability to focus completely inwardly for a brief time interval. Team sports, on the other hand, require the ability to integrate with many other players continuously over a game that lasts for hours.

Before UST, there could be no understanding of the differences between selling Products and Services. As we've seen in earlier chapters of this book, the processes of selling Products and Services are very different from each other, and *these differences affect the skills and traits needed for success.* The Human Resource issues of Hiring, Training, and Employee Relations are the subject of this chapter.

Hiring:

HR managers are trained to make sure that the personality of the recruit matches the culture of the company. It's equally important to make sure the personality of the recruit matches the nature of the Product/Service entity they are selling.

HR managers are familiar with dozens of "standard" personality profiling tools: The Enneagram, Myers-Briggs, Holland Interest… the list goes on. Unfortunately, there is not yet a single test that specifically differentiates between the personality traits needed for selling Services versus Products.

Let's review those personality traits as a first step to your department identifying what your pre-hire testing program should be.

In Chapter 8, we compared two snippets of dialogue from the sales pitch of two salespeople, one selling cars, and the other bespoke suites. The car salesperson, as with any Product salesperson, is selling something with "attributes" and tries to mention as many features and benefits as possible in the hopes of hitting a hot button that will cause the buyer to make final selection and payment. The salesperson has lots to talk about and must carry the conversation. It's unlikely that every (or even most) buyers will ask if the car has a sway bar or not. The salesperson must bring it up, perhaps even explaining its function, so that the buyer can see the benefit. Product salespeople have to be good talkers. They have to have a personality type that is undaunted by indifference or even silence on the part of the buyer. Buyer silence doesn't have an impact on Product sales, since even a buyer who does nothing but listen can still make final selection and pay. The Product salesperson must methodically recite the statements and questions of the sales script. Although they must listen actively, they are primarily listening for "landmarks" on the convergence roadmap and for what are called "buy signs"—the indications that it's time to start closing.

The tailor, on the other hand, succeeds by listening for the desired benefits that will define the features of the suit that will be made once the client's other service inputs (fabric, measurements, etc.) are received. The tailor has to be a prober and a listener, not a reciter. With every answer that is received, the salesperson's direction diverges to add a new detail to the final proposal.

True, a tailor who has been making suits for 30 years has probably heard it all before, but each suit is a new engagement, and each one starts from nothing.[1] Until the client opens up and offers service inputs, the suit has no form. It's imperative that a Service salesperson be able to elicit service inputs from the client, otherwise the proposal can never be written. Service salespeople have to be prepared to probe and improvise to follow the conversation into new regions.

The Service salesperson has to listen actively, thinking about what the client is saying and making mental notes about the outcomes the client wants to see. Those are the benefits that will dictate the features. The more the client talks, the more detailed and useful the proposal will be. Not everybody is a "listener," so it falls to the HR specialist to identify the listeners and the talkers and to know when each is required based on the offering they will represent.

The last chapter explained that Product selling uses a sales script that systematically follows a path from broad, "open ended"

---

[1] My tailor hunts for meat here in Manitoba where game is plentiful—everything from turkeys to moose. Many of his clients are hunters, and he's made a surprising number of suits and tuxedos out of camouflage fabric.

questions of the needs analysis to the narrow, "closed ended" questions of the close. Not everybody is comfortable following a verbatim script. Both Products and Productized Services follow this sales process. Therefore, the hiring manager needs to know if the company's offering is a regular Service or a Productized Service. One is sold like a Service and the other like a Product.

As a sales manager selling a Productized Service, I can remember telling trainees, "Say it exactly like it says in the book." Sometimes a new recruit would want to deviate, essentially paraphrasing what the script said. I learned over time that those variations didn't sell as much as the original script, and so I required they do it the "right" way.

I had people quit because they weren't comfortable following a script or who insisted it was better to improvise than risk sounding "canned." And I lost some who just weren't willing to put in the hard work needed to make a script sound natural. I had hired the wrong people and was now wasting time trying to train them. Looking back, I realize that what was wrong was that I had hired people with good credentials (job history, temperament) for selling Services, but *I* didn't understand that what we were selling was a Productized Service.[2]

Eventually, I learned to add questions to the interview about their readiness to memorize sales tracts and their willingness to adopt a belief that *their* approaches might not be as effective as those developed by a company that had been successful for 40 years.

---

[2] Because the term didn't exist yet. Because there were no correct definitions for Products or Services yet. Because I hadn't created the SIPS grid yet.

Service salespeople, on the other hand, need to encourage open conversation and be patient enough to give the client a chance to respond. It can be difficult for Service buyers to explain what they want. A Product salesperson can show examples of existing Products that allow an effortless response from the buyer: "I like the comfort of the van, but I need something with more cargo area." A Service buyer will have an outcome in mind but may have trouble putting it into words: "We want visitors to our church to get a soaring feeling when they look at it from the outside or when they're in the main sanctuary. But we don't want it to be tall or pointy. So, soar-y, but not pointy. Do you know what I mean?" Sometimes, the client is sharing those needs with outsiders for the first time and has to hunt for the right words.

I can remember taking new Service salespeople with me on sales calls and thinking to myself, "Shut up, shut up, shut up! You have to let them speak." There are people who are uncomfortable with the silence that comes when a client is trying to articulate an answer to question. Those are the wrong people for Services and for Service/Product hybrids.

As the HR specialist, you need to understand what your sales team is representing and to be able to figure out if you need "good talkers" or "good listeners." *Use the SIPS grid to determine what your sales requirements are.*

Employee Relations is also part of the HR manager's responsibility and preventing the discord that comes from having a staff filled with people who continuously object to prescribed methods, such as "script following."

Consider a person who has moved from a successful position selling Services to a new position selling Products—or vice versa, or even selling Productized Services to Services. That person will be frustrated by poor sales but not understand that they needed to completely change their selling approach. Frustration can manifest itself as anger at the company, because, from the salesperson's standpoint, the only thing that has changed is the company they work for. They might feel the offering is not competitive (when it is), or that the sales training isn't effective (when it is), or that their boss is an idiot (when I'm not).

I'm amused by recruitment ads for Service salespeople that insist they want "3 years selling in XYZ industry," without also requiring a successful history selling *Services* in that industry. Take the transportation industry, for example: a salesperson who has been successful selling lubricants to trucking companies would probably also do well selling tires. But that same person would have no understanding of how to sell logistics services, access to cross-docking facilities, or vehicle modification.

To be clear, the lubricant salesperson would have a better understanding of what those services are than a person with no trucking experience, but that understanding would not translate to an ability to *sell* those services. In this case, it would be easier to train an experienced Services salesperson in vehicle and trucking issues. That salesperson would know nothing about the industry coming into the job, but they would have a "gut" understanding that their goal is to "get something" from the client rather than just "tell something."[3]

The form of my sales scripts barely changed as I moved across Service industries, but they remained effective regardless of vertical. All that changed were the industry issues.

- I'm calling from Icon Health. We're a full-service market research firm specializing in prescription pharmaceuticals, and we have extensive experience in oncology drug development, both solid and liquid tumors, including direct treatments and support drugs. The reason I'm calling is I see you are in Phase Three trials for two new colorectal molecules, and we helped bring Vectibix and Erbitux to market. *I was wondering how we would go about being considered by your team for future projects?*

- I'm calling from Icon Engineering. We're a Manufacturing Engineering firm that focuses on the flexible packaging industry: printing, converting, and filling. If you're not familiar with our work, I'll say we take a holistic approach, with a team that includes chemists who specialize in inks and solvents and adhesives, plant architects, tool-and-die makers, operator trainers, and a North American-based repair crew that knows both European and Asian equipment. The reason I'm calling is we'd like to be considered as a supplier of engineering services, and *I was wondering what would be the best way for us to introduce ourselves to your team?*

---

[3] The goal of this book is to help them understand why that is so, and how to maximize the process.

What I brought with me to these sales roles were a natural curiosity and great listening skills—things that are hard to teach. What each employer provided to me were an understanding of their industry and the services they offered—things that are easy to teach.[4]

The HR Manager should take the time to examine a candidate's previous company and understand where the *previous* company's offering fell in the SIPS grid. Remember, when moving horizontally or diagonally across the SIPS grid, the sales approach changes. When moving vertically, the sales approach remains the same.

When I look at people who have enjoyed long and successful sales careers, I note that, although they moved from company to company, they have always made vertical moves along the SIPS grid.

As part of the onboarding process, you need to make sure that new sales hires are aware if they have changed offering categories.

Training:

Being a good listener is just a starting point for the new Service salesperson hire. The sales leadership must work with the HR department to ensure that every new hire doesn't have to reinvent the wheel.

Trainees need to learn about the capabilities of the company and how those capabilities are combined after the initial meeting

---

[4] You'd be stunned to see how little technical knowledge is required to get a prospect to agree to a statement of capabilities. I've booked meetings to discuss being a service provider with manufacturers of arthroscopic surgical equipment with a knowledge base gleaned from a Wikipedia article. There is a huge difference between knowing how to do something and knowing how to talk about doing something. I have made a career of talking the talk and representing professionals who could walk the walk.

to create a solution. The new hire should get sample scripts of how to lead a discussion and a starter set of open-ended questions that are applicable to the industry. They should also get coaching from a senior rep as to what the key concerns of the day are. As I moved from Healthcare consulting to IT consulting to Market Research consulting to Engineering consulting, I had to re-learn each industry's issues and catch phrases.

A Product salesperson's training manual holds three kinds of information:

- Detailed information about each Product's features and benefits, and how they combine to provide a solution to a client's needs.
- A differential-diagnosis-style sales script to bring the customer to a "buy-able" solution.
- Closing techniques to gain payment for the Product the client has chosen.

A Service salesperson's training manual also holds three kinds of information:

- Detailed information about Service capabilities and how they combine to provide solutions to clients in that industry.
- A basic discussion guide (industry issues, open-ended exploratory questions, POSI list). This guide gives them the knowledge base they need to direct a conversation that will elicit POSI, so the proposal-writing team can create a "buy-able" solution.

- Closing techniques to get the client to choose and pay for the proposal that is being offered.

The Human Resources Manager needs to select training strategies (role play, manuals, etc.) that will prepare new salespeople for the sales environment they will experience. Products favor understanding and memorization. Services favor understanding and improvisation.

As an HR Manager, *it's your responsibility to understand what your recruits will be selling.* Will it be a Service or a Product, or a Productized Service that needs a Product salesperson's sales skill, or a Product/Service Hybrid that looks like a Product but needs a salesperson more suited to Services?

In the real world, though, some companies don't sell just one type of thing or another. If Products and Productized Services need a Product salesperson's mentality, and Services and S/P Hybrids need a Service salesperson's mentality, what kind of person should be hired when the company's offering is a mix of Products *and* Services?

Answer: A Service salesperson.

There was no waffling or discussion on that answer. Here's why:

When Products and Services are sold at the same time, the Products are always part of the "solution space" found in the Service proposal. It's very difficult to embed a Service within a Product, because, by definition, a Product is made without service inputs. When a Service is embedded as part of a Product quotation, the result is an S/P Hybrid, which must be sold the same way a Service is.

The only exception is when the Service is first productized. In that case, the hybrid consists of a Product and a Productized Service, which is sold the same way as two Products together.

Here's an example: A shopper purchases 50 bundles of roof shingles at a local building supply store and needs to get them home. The shopper can self-service that need (assuming they own a truck), or they can purchase a delivery service from the store. The delivery service is priced as follows:

- Delivery within 5 miles: $10 per each 100 lbs or portion thereof
- Delivery between 5 and 10 miles: $25 per each 100 lbs or portion thereof
- Delivery more than 10 miles: Contact delivery manager for a quotation

The rationale for this pricing system is that there are numerous trucks circulating in the city on regular routes, but delivery outside the city requires scheduling a special trip, perhaps coordinating multiple deliveries to the remote area.

For nearby deliveries, the delivery Service is productized and can be effortlessly sold as an add-on by the Product (shingles) salesperson. No additional expertise is needed to sell *a productized* delivery service. The shingles salesperson can accept final selection (e.g., "between 5 and 10 miles") and payment.

Custom delivery is a Service requiring different expertise. The delivery manager doesn't need to know about the difference between 20-year and 25-year shingles. The delivery manager is a logistics person and needs to understand how delivery service inputs like location, weight, volume, and timing all affect delivery costs. Once an un-productized Service is bundled to a Product, a Service salesperson is required.

We are in an age where software can automate many of the "manual" HR functions like scheduling and tracking certification updates. I believe the folks in charge of *Human Capital Management* and *Workforce Management* have a vital role to play in the overall Big-M Marketing strategy of the company as well as in the tactical execution of Small-M Marketing. At a time when surgeons turn part of their process over to robots, selling may be the last truly *human* activity, and it's imperative that Human Resource managers understand where in the SIPS grid their company's offering falls. Without that understanding, they can't guide sales managers to hire the right people. To reiterate page 78, historically, more than 50% of new sales hires failed in their new roles. New tools, like the SIPS grid, give you the power to hire more effectively.

Chapter Eleven

Final Thoughts, Invitations, and Final Exam

Sampson and Froehle's Unified Services Theory has changed the way we think about Products and Services. For the first time, we are able to discuss their true differences in a precise and consistent manner. UST serves as our scalpel and our microscope.

Applying UST has opened my eyes to fundamental differences in business operations: We can now see that Product providers add value to their offerings before the sales process begins, but Service providers can't start adding value until after the sales process ends.

I now understand why I always felt lost, and I can see where previous researchers lost their way: It's not a Product/Service dichotomy, and it's not an infinite spectrum of intangibility. There are exactly four variations of offering: Products, Services,

Productized Services, and Product/Service Hybrids. My SIPS grid tells us whether an offering needs to be sold like a Product or like a Service.

From a business practitioner's standpoint, UST gives managers practical advice. We can see that, at every step in the sales pipeline, from prospecting to closing, the process for selling Services differs from the process for selling Products. These differences have ramifications for the HR department, for Sales Managers, for Salespeople, for the Marketing Department, and for the C-Suite.

From an academic standpoint, UST allows us to conduct research without being confused about whether an offering is a Product or a Service. For the first time, we have operative definitions of Services and Products. Suddenly, Service Science is truly a science, where researchers around the world have a consistent benchmark against which to standardize and compare their work.

This is the service reboot, the first sales and marketing book in the post-UST world. I understand it's just the beginning of the conversation. Every reader will have their own take on my work. There will be arguments against what I've written and case studies that support it. I'd love to hear your thoughts. Please write to me at David@ServiceReboot.com. *I promise to respond.*

I'm currently working on specialized versions of this book for individual verticals. Eventually, I hope to see focused books offering best sales and marketing practices as they apply to Law, Engineering, Education, Logistics, Healthcare, and insert-your-Service-vertical-here. If you are involved in sales or marketing at your firm and would like to be part of that research, please reach out: David@ServiceReboot.com.

Finally, I offer consulting services at very reasonable rates. If you would like help implementing the lessons of this book in your organization, shoot me a note and tell me about your specific situation. Remember, I'm the guy who literally wrote the book on this stuff.

So here's your final exam to see what you learned from the book:

Some consulting services are available as packages:

- *Win More Business by Writing Fewer Proposals Part One—Sales Theory for Professionals*
- *Win More Business by Writing Fewer Proposals Part Two—Role Play Drills for Professionals*
- *The Service/Product Dichotomy—Overview for the C-Suite*
- *Lectures for Organizations and Conferences*
- *Your Latent Business Part One—Reactivating Those Stale Business Cards Gathering Dust in Your Desk*
- *Your Latent Business Part Two—Grow Your Billings With Existing Clients*

Write to me if you'd like more information: David@ServiceReboot.com

What's wrong with that last section in italics? I've deliberately made my offer of consulting services weak. There are at least four problems with it. How could it have been stronger? What is poorly done based on the lessons of UST? Everything you need to score 100% is in the book. Need a hint? Use the SIPS grid.

Thank you for reading my book.

Did you enjoy this book? Did you find it useful? Please recommend it to your colleagues, and write a post about it on LinkedIn.

I write updates periodically on ServiceReboot.com. Register there for free bonus chapters and to download the free Service Reboot workbook.

You can follow me on LinkedIn: www.linkedin.com/in/davidselch.

About the Author

D avid Selch is an expert in the sales and marketing of Services and complex Service-Product hybrids, and has personally closed contracts at the head offices of 30 companies in the Fortune 100. He's led teams representing a diverse variety of services that includes research design, software development, educa- tion, healthcare, financing, insurance, fitness, and engineering. Thousands of professionals have benefited from his sales training.

Mr. Selch holds an MBA from the University of Leicester in the U.K. and a BSc in Molecular Biology. He takes a scientific approach to marketing and feels all business decisions should be evidence-based. As he puts it, "We've all got budgets to beat. I don't care how you've always done it. Let's figure out what always works."

Selch has been recognized for bringing a sense of humor to serious writing; the CBC broadcast *Before Free Swim,* his comedy about the recurrence of bigotry. As one reviewer put it, "I like the quality of Mr. Selch's voice: wry, insightful, often humorous—but highly effective." His business students at University of Winnipeg give him high marks for making dry and difficult concepts "fascinating and funny."

David explains he resides with his wife Debbie in Winnipeg, Manitoba, the coldest and windiest city on earth, (550 miles further north than Chicago). They've dragged their kids across the continent to see the northern lights, a total solar eclipse, meteor showers, a transit of Venus, and Pluto, Mickey's friend.

Follow David Selch on Linkedin: www.linkedin.com/in/davidselch